Jean Harris

MW01097165

And Lead Us Not Into Dysfunction

And Lead Us Not Into Dysfunction

The Good, The Bad, and The Ugly of Church
Organizations and Their Leaders

MICHAEL P. FRIDAY

WIPF & STOCK · Eugene, Oregon

AND LEAD US NOT INTO DYSFUNCTION
The Good, The Bad, and The Ugly of Church Organizations and Their Leaders

Wipf & Stock
An Imprint of Wipf and Stock Publishers
199 W. 8th Ave., Suite 3
Eugene, OR 97401

www.wipfandstock.com

PAPERBACK ISBN: 978-1-5326-3673-8
HARDCOVER ISBN: 978-1-5326-3675-2
EBOOK ISBN: 978-1-5326-3674-5

Manufactured in the U.S.A.   DECEMBER 19, 2017

Dedication

From me:
For Vivienne, my wife,
Love of my life, most of my life.
To God who leads in mysterious ways.
For Vivienne: patient, generous, anchor, friend, faithful.
For Vivienne, who has borne with me all of my growth as a leader.
For the congregations that have given me the scope for growth as a leader.
For young pastors and seminarians who need not stumble as I did as I grew as a leader.
For my colleagues, burdened, battered, burned—yet blessed—with the gift of leadership.
For my family in the faith, everywhere, trying to make sense of your leaders.
For leaders everywhere, trying to do your best with those you serve.
For Christians, trying to better order and organize their churches.
For Clara and Rochford, long since gone; they first led me.
For Davewin, Rhaema, Jeremy, and Eva.
For Joan, Alden, Arthur, and Tori.
For anyone, curious.
Thank you!

The stories told in this book are true. The names, places, and circumstances have been changed (except where otherwise noted) to protect the innocent . . . and the other kind.

Contents

Preface

MY EARLIEST MEMORIES DATE back to more than fifty years. All of those years have been lived in the life of the church: first as a child attending worship on Sunday mornings with my family in a little rural church, then returning in the afternoon for Sunday school. The total distance to church was four miles round-trip, which we often walked. At age thirteen, one year after beginning secondary school, my family moved to the city, and to a city church. I got more deeply involved in youth fellowship meetings, eventually leading them. I moved on to involvement in my denomination's regional youth department. Meanwhile, I joined the youth choir (which was that church's only choir), eventually directing it. There being musical instruments in this city church, I took up learning music, and in short or-der, alternated playing organ and piano on Sundays along with the church musician; she was the one who taught me music.

Still in my mid-teens, I served the church as Sunday School Secretary. Around age fifteen, after my pastors helped me clarify that I was sensing a divine call to ministry of some kind, I attended a local seminary part-time while still in high school. Immediately following high school, I left for a Bible college abroad, then to university and seminary, concurrently.

I returned home to my first pastorate, and was immediately plunged into denominational leadership at a national level. I was appointed pastor of a church which I served for five years. When I resigned that pastorate, I was the twelfth pastor (including missionary and lay pastors) who was resigning. At that time, the church was only twenty-one years old. No pas-tor, either before me or after me, up until this time of writing nearly thirty years later, has served that church as long as five years. (Two or three lay persons, whose only task was to preach on Sundays, have each exceeded five years.) This is to demonstrate the crucible in which my pastoral and congregational learnings of leadership were forged. It was a very difficult assignment, no fault of the good folk that constituted the congregation. The fault—as I understand it now but did not then—was precisely with the way the church was constituted, the failure of its founders to clarify values, vision, and mission. That failure extended into many other matters that went straight to the heart of leadership, leadership structure, leadership relationships, and the underdevelopment of a leadership vision that the young church experienced over its entire sixteen years before my arrival. I have since learned that this dear little congregation, despite growing by 300 percent in membership during my time, is not unique in its leadership travails.

From this crucible has ensued twenty-nine more years of service in congregations and denominations in three different international locations. A five-year stint as a police chaplain afforded a refreshing, timely, and different kind of experience which has also contributed significantly to who I have become, and how I have offered, inspired, and engaged in leadership in congregational and denominational life.

It is said that when a man boasts of having thirty years' experience, the listener might do well to ask a few probing questions. This, because the hearer might discover that all the speaker has is really one year's experience, thirty times! Because of the nature of my work in churches and the extent of my travels, I have become intimate with nearly thirty churches during the course of my life, whether as a member, a musician, a student pastor, a settled pastor, or an interim pastor. These churches span about ten different cultures, some ethnic, some social, some cultural, some international. As one who has been involved in a variety of leader positions in church life for more than forty years, I have often wondered whether the sense of déjà vu I experience time and again is new learning or experience, or whether I am simply having the same old single experience one more time!

Although a group of leaders is often loosely referred to as "leadership," leadership—as this book discloses—is more a state that exists between two or more persons who share a relationship in which they are meant to encourage one another towards the fulfillment of some goal, or some worthy cause. Leadership does not necessarily repose *only* in one or more select and exclusive persons in a given group; and the word, "leadership," is not necessarily interchangeable with *a group of leaders* in a group. This mistake, subtle as it is, is only one of those many mistakes that create problems with leaders, leadership, and leading, in church life.

I have seen the church at work from both sides of the fence, both as parishioner and pastoral leader. I have seen it from the congregational floor as well as the denominational balcony. I have lived it. I have experienced it. I have been pastor of churches with double-digit membership, one with four digits, with several triple-digit ones in between. I have been pastor of white congregations and black congregations. I have pastored in the city and in the village. I have been welcomed and loved, and I have been scorned and dismissed. I have done some things quite right, and botched up a few other things quite badly. Somehow, I think I've become some kind of authority on church leadership. When Jesus taught his disciples to pray, he included the lesson, "And lead us not into temptation." But somehow, from the experiences I have seen, lived, and heard, I've found myself often praying, "And lead us not into dysfunction." This book is written with the sincere hope that it contributes immensely to dysfunction-avoidance.

Finally, all of the stories told in this book are true. I am grateful to the colleagues who have shared their experiences, friendships, and lives with me, and to whose experiences I have added mine to tell these tales. The names of the people in each story have been changed. The names of organizations, along with their locations and some of the circumstances that can make them identifiable to others (and perhaps, in some cases, even to the people themselves) have also been changed. This, we suppose, avoids leading the author into defamation. None of the stories told in this book, regardless of how outlandish, are fabricated; that of course, could be tantamount to leading the reader into deception. Truth is still stranger than fiction! All of the issues in this book are pursued with the hope that neither the readers, nor their church, or denomination, or church organization, or any other organization to which they might apply these principles, would be led into dysfunction. Instead, my hope is that all such entities would be delivered from organizational and leadership evil—of which I have become certain from my lifelong observations, there is already too much in the church.

Amen, so let it be!

Acknowledgments

I ALWAYS KNEW THAT I would write a book. I had actually started one in my own handwriting (before the days of computers—I never owned a typewriter) and had arrived at chapter 6 before deciding that this was neither the time nor the approach. However, when I did my first postgraduate course of study—a Master of Philosophy degree by thesis only—my academic supervisor advised that I write for publication. I did write that thesis with the intent to have it published, but let us just say that life intervened.

When I went on to a doctoral degree, I recalled the advice of my master's degree supervisor, to the extent that in fact, a part of my dissertation was a one-hundred-page book outline, with the full intent to flesh it all out and produce a book. Even though my two academic supervisors (one of whom was the late, great Haddon Robinson, that celebrated American expositor, preacher, homiletician, and teacher) were very happy at what they read, life intervened again, and nothing went to press.

A decade later, I returned to the classroom to pursue postgraduate work in organizational leadership. This helped me focus my passions and concerns; I knew this was the time and topic. Therefore, I want to thank Neville Callam, former General Secretary of the Baptist World Alliance, who first encouraged me way back in 1995: "Write for publication." I finally did, Neville!

I thank my friend, Karl Henlin, one of the smartest people I know, for the hours upon hours of argument and discussion that have pervaded our lengthy and rich friendship, and which have contributed to the resolve to write this book. His intellectual twin is my other dear friend, Clinton Chisholm, who—along with Karl—read the first five chapters of this book.

Clinton's fulsome responses, and Karl's uncontrollable laughter at some of my stories therein were sufficient affirmations that I was on the right track!

Among the many congregations and church entities that have inspired and shaped me in my journey toward this book are the Baptist Union of Trinidad and Tobago, into which I was birthed a child, a Christian, and a minister, and the Jamaica Baptist Union, which birthed me theologically, professionally, and intellectually. Both, along with sojourns in the American Baptist Churches of Connecticut, and the American Baptist Churches of Nebraska, have made invaluable contributions to my growth in leadership, leadership critique, and leadership dissatisfaction which—like dissatisfaction in so many other spheres of life—goaded, prodded, and nudged me to the conviction that there had to be better ways in the pursuit of excellence.

My friend, Tom Wiles, the Executive Minister of the American Baptist Churches of Rhode Island, along with the region's Ministers' Council, sat with me one spring day in 2015 to critique this book in its outline and embryonic stage; their insights were helpful. My cohorts in the Class of 2015 from Eastern University's Master of Arts in Organizational Leadership degree program, as well as all the professors, deserve my gratitude. Danel Payne, the Administrative Assistant at the Union Baptist Church of Swissvale, PA, managed to retain her sanity while bringing my diagrams and figures to their final shape.

Finally, my wife, Vivienne, married me back in 1983 when I was a novice leader. For staying with me to this point of lesser underdevelopment, and through the many experiences that might have made lesser mortals jump ship and never return to church, I owe her the utmost gratitude. For the grace, peace, calm, and anchor she is and has been to me, I crown her champion! She is a leader; and perhaps my most influential and transformational life-leader.

Undergirding all of this is the abiding faith of my parents, grandparents, and ancestors, and the God of grace and love they trusted, and to whom they introduced me, and to whom they have returned. I would not know leadership in this way, had I not known, by faith, this God, to whom all praise and thanks are returned.

PART I

It Is Eleven O'clock Sunday Morning; Do You Know Who Your Church Is?

I know your deeds; you have a reputation of being alive, but you are dead.
—*Rev 3:1, NIV*

I know your deeds, that you are neither cold nor hot. I wish you were either one or the other!
—*Rev 3:15, NIV*

I know your deeds . . . Yet I hold this against you: You have forsaken your first love.
—*Rev 2:2, 4, NIV*

Chapter 1

Four Churches You May Know

AT FIRST GLANCE, YOUR church may look like a church. You know that church very well. There are some things about your church, though, that either worry you or give you pause, or create searching questions for you. Nagging questions. Disconcerting questions. Something about your church isn't quite right. You know it deep down, but you can't quite place your proverbial finger on exactly what it might be. You may not realize it, but your mind and spirit are really prodding you toward processing organizational questions about your church. Some of those questions touch on the leaders, others on the members; but overall, they all regard the way your church is organized, and who your church really is. Questions about how your church functions or does not function are questions about organization. Above all, though, your questions about your church arise from your particular understanding about church, which may or may not be Tom, Dick, Harry, or Mary's understanding about church. It all boils down to the frame through which you are viewing your church, and whether your church is healthy or unhealthy.

There are good churches and, unfortunately, there are also bad churches. Of the bad kinds, there are many, by many different names. You might probably know one or more of the four churches in this chapter; well, not necessarily by name or location, but you probably know four churches either exactly like these or very much like these. You probably know a church that is an exclusive social club; another, which is a kingdom; still another that is a bureaucracy; and one more, a museum.

THE EXCLUSIVE SOCIAL CLUB: CITY EDGE CHURCH

You may not want to know it, but your church may be an *exclusive social club*. Churches are always in danger of becoming exclusive social clubs, draped in biblical curtains. More churches have succumbed to this threat than realize it. Perhaps your church, or one you know, is already an exclusive social club. Now, don't toss the book out of the window in disgust just yet—keep on reading!

City Edge Church had been declining for decades; yet, many of the members who still remained, loved being there. City Edge has had an extensive—and alarming—turnover of pastors in the last thirty years. Problems began for Glenroy Hughes, City Edge's most recent pastoral alumnus, when he urged the members to understand that, if they were to be a congregation that was true to its calling to imitate Christ, they therefore did not exist to serve themselves but instead to serve their community. This, among other things, annoyed some of City Edge's leaders, and started the tide toward Hughes's eventual dismissal. This dismissal was not occasioned by a congregational vote, as required by the fledgling church's bylaws, but by the church's deacons, accustomed to doing their own thing, while enjoying their special club status as "deacons for life." They enjoyed this status whether or not they continued to be fit to be deacons, and whether or not their actions injured or displeased the congregation.

When City Edge called Glenroy Hughes as pastor, it was clear that the deacons and members had the hope that the church's membership would grow; indeed, Hughes's own family members constituted a full 20 percent of the church's usual Sunday attendance, and his teenaged children were often the only ones of that demographic present. Shortly after Hughes's arrival, new visitors began to stay—at least, some of them—as they discerned desirable change beginning to percolate through the church, due to their pastor's leadership attitudes and initiatives. However, it was these same attitudes and initiatives for change which began to challenge the old deacons' self-perceived power, making it clear that were City Edge to grow in any way, power shifts had to happen and old stumbling blocks had to give way to new vision.

It was Hughes's submission to the church board of a written proposal for changes in City Edge's congregational life, as well as ministry and management, that placed him on the fast track to dismissal. Before the board could even meet to hear him and discuss the document he delivered for their contemplation ahead of a meeting, the deacons and other leaders' easy suspicion and paranoia were piqued, and blunted any hope for objectivity in those discussions. The discussions never happened. Some of the younger deacons and other leaders understood, and were quite supportive of, Hughes's initiative; they believed it to be not only the reason new visitors were coming and staying, but saw it as the way to City Edge's new and bright future.

While all of this was happening, within his first four months at City Edge, Hughes was already processing twelve people who requested membership. Those twelve would have increased City Edge's membership by 80 percent! Processing certain categories of new members included an interview by the deacons. For some reason, the deacons failed to meet after Hughes advised them of the twelve applicants. Time and again, Hughes would remind the deacons of the need to meet the twelve. Five months passed, each with several reminders. No meeting happened. Gradually, seven of the twelve left and went elsewhere. Re-reading the bylaws one day, Hughes discovered an oversight he had made and realized that the application status of the remaining five did not require the deacons' approval; but only pastoral approval and presentation to the congregation for their welcome.

Ironically and unbelievably, it was the Sunday when Hughes attempted to present and welcome the five to the membership of City Edge that all hell broke loose. The old deacons (along with a couple of their younger supporters) objected, interrupted, and destroyed the worship service, despite the pleadings of George Conrad, one of City Edge's denominational leaders whom Hughes had invited, and who had a long history of interventions with City Edge over the past decades. Nevertheless, the old deacons prevailed. The five membership applicants, though accepted into membership by the remainder of the bewildered congregation, were, by the following Sunday, worshipping elsewhere, because, by the end of that week, news had circulated that Hughes had received a letter from a lawyer, retained by City Edge's deacons, advising him of his dismissal and warning of trespassing, arrest, and prosecution if he should return to the church premises.

City Edge's leaders—though not all of them—preferred to squander the arrival of congregational renewal and membership growth rather than make way for the marvelous change that was seeking to break in. Curiously, they desired the church to grow, but evidently did not want any new members! Their new pastor and the remaining five prospective members represented to these old persons (along with a couple of younger leaders, relatives, and supporters) a threat to the status quo. The new pastor and prospective members signaled a significant change in City Edge's very nature, and the end of the congregation's inertia and insularity. But, quite sadly, City Edge preferred to remain an exclusive social club—and a very *small* one at that—rather than become a viable and effervescent congregation of Jesus Christ in a neighborhood that desperately needed a healthy presence of and witness to Christ. Conrad, the denominational representative, told the deacons and other leaders that day that they just squandered their very last chance of becoming a healthy congregation, and that he, too, was finished with them.

THE KINGDOM: OCEAN VIEW FELLOWSHIP

Perhaps your church is nothing like City Edge. Perhaps it is a more sophisticated version of an exclusive social club, minus the rancor and obvious disease as City Edge's. Perhaps it is in no near danger at all of being or becoming an exclusive social club. Perhaps, though, it may be a *kingdom*, or in danger of becoming a kingdom.

Terry Fellowes has been Ocean View Fellowship's pastor from the church's inception. Fellowes planted the church in a depressed side of town several years ago, and then years later moved the congregation into a spanking new building on a bustling side of town, though not quite the suburbs. The congregation grew, to the point of becoming one of Ocean View City's premier churches. Terry Fellowes had the last say in everything, and nearly always the first word, too. He led with a strong arm, and few persons would cross him or his opinions. Yet, the congregation kept growing. Reverend Fellowes had a charming personality despite how brusque he could be when laying down the law.

Over time, though, prominent persons began leaving Ocean View. Some left because they no longer felt they could toe the line, or challenge Fellowes; some were either shown the door or felt such onerous requirements made of them that persuaded them that they could not stay. Others were consistently locking horns with Fellowes. A large number left because they were threatened for inadequate financial giving and pressured to tithe. Rather than being pastorally engaged or compassionately encouraged, they felt angrily confronted, and publicly humiliated. Some were convinced that they were excommunicated; and some others, believing that they were delivered an ultimatum, chose to leave.

Ocean View had, over the years, developed a cadre of promising young leaders, many of whom attended Bible colleges in preparation for pastoral leadership. Every one of them, in one fashion or another, found himself embroiled in some kind of altercation or parting of ways with Fellowes. Fellowes had no meaningful relationship with his denominational colleagues, or with the other pastors in town. Soon, people began to describe his members as "Fellowes's Forlorn Fellows" and other less complimentary names. They described Fellowes as King Fellowes, and Ocean View as Fellowes's Kingdom.

Forty years after it was first established as a promising congregation, Ocean View Fellowship has never planted a new congregation. Some of the members who attended Bible colleges went on to pastor and even plant other churches. People who have known Ocean View all its life agree that, for all the human capital and the varieties of gifts they brought to Ocean View, if things were different, it could have been the lead church, not only in the entire county, but also in the entire state. They are convinced that it could also have been a national exemplar. They consider it lamentable for Ocean View that so many of their former members are now ensconced in several bustling congregations in and around Ocean View. Currently at Ocean View, there remains room for many more, not only in the several empty spaces in the sanctuary pews, but also in the congregation's circle of leaders. It is a circle that still comprises only Fellowes and a few hand-picked yes-men and yes-women.

Perhaps you are saying, "Phew! Thank God my church is nothing like Ocean View's Fellowes's Kingdom!" But kingdoms do not come in only one size, shape or form, and they are often far more subtle than Ocean View, with a serving of sugar and spice sprinkled in. There are many congregational kingdoms where all of the "subjects" are actually very happy, and the "king," even happier, but where that king—not necessarily Jesus—is lord of all. Perchance, your church is not a kingdom, or at risk of being one. But maybe—just maybe—your church might be a *bureaucracy.*

THE BUREAUCRACY: PORTLAND HILL CHAPEL

Everyone would like to claim that their church is well-organized. Maybe your church is; maybe it isn't. But if it is organized, it should be *well-organized*—not just *merely* or *barely* organized. It is entirely possible for churches to be over-organized, to the extent that the organization becomes onerous. The organization becomes smothered in and bogged down by some measures and streamlining that hinder the organization's smooth flow, leaving its members confused and unhappy. Those systems, even though they exist and have been crafted for facilitating efficiency, become the proverbial red tape if they do not really facilitate efficiency.

Portland Hill Chapel is a two-hundred-year-old congregation. For decades, the church functioned under an organizational structure that divided their vital functions into boards: a board of education, a board of deacons, a board of stewardship, and more. Each board was required to report to the general board monthly. There was a time when Portland Hill's membership broke the four hundred mark; and there was a time when the boards worked. In recent years, however, Portland Hill's membership—like so many other congregations—dipped below one hundred in attendance on Sunday mornings. The church decided, partly because of its member-ship decline, to re-examine its structure and to change it.

For several years, a task force met and discussed the church's realities and studied documents. They observed that their general board meetings got bogged down in minutiae regarding the work of each of the church's boards and committees, and that little or no time was left for visioning and dreaming about the big picture and future of ministry. Further, the gen-eral board meetings had swollen to a very large group of persons, almost a combination of all of the church's boards. More people appeared to be involved in these meetings, but fewer people appeared to be really engaging in ministry. Often nothing in ministry happened unless the general board approved it; the subordinate boards were required, in many cases, to await the general board's approval. Something had to change.

After several long months of investigations and meetings and deliber-ations, the task force recommended a new organizational structure to Port-land Hill Chapel. The model promised movement away from bureaucracy toward efficiency. It did away with boards, and instead named ministries. Each ministry would be served by several ministry teams as needed, and all the ministry teams together would, by and large, undertake all the church's work, ministry, and mission. There was only one small problem; actually, there were five. First, there was a total of fifty-five ministries, while the ac-tive membership of the church had shrunk to about seventy-five. Second, some of the ministries had no leaders appointed (and remained so for well over a year after the church began utilizing the model), including the ever-important spiritual development ministry. Third, about half of the ministry teams were understaffed or not staffed at all, even if a ministry leader was appointed. Fourth, many of the ministry teams' areas of focus were so in-frequently required or now irrelevant or not needed, that it appeared to be a waste of talent appointing persons to that ministry team. Fifth, in addition to the foregoing personnel gaps, because the ministry leaders/coordinators were no longer required to be members of the new church council, there arose much confusion about key contact persons, and accountability; and generally, communication became more complex, and many in the congregation reported that the new model was confusing. It did not help that a new category of council member was created: a "messenger" from each of the ministries to the council. These messengers were to bring to the council the concerns of the ministries. The idea was to relieve the council of the minutiae of each ministry's development and plans, and to endow the council with the freedom from all of that, so they might be focus on future ministry.

But while some of that did happen, this model had the opposite effect of reducing oversight of ministries. It placed distance between the ministry leaders and the church's council. This had the effect of actually reducing the church members' engagement in ministry, admittedly, also due to the members' habit over the years, of watching boards and the pastor do the work! Even some of Portland Hill's leaders thought that the old model was not only less confusing but more desirable!

About a year after the model was commissioned, Portland Hill Chapel came to the stark realization that, in their bid to become a more ministry-athletic church, they had actually stumbled into an organizational conundrum that made them more bureaucratic, even though the intent was the opposite. Still, Portland Hill's leaders decided to forge ahead, confident that with time and better communication, the structure would work.

THE MUSEUM: OLDBURY COMMUNITY TEMPLE

You may find that your church or one you know has made an attempt recently to change some old and unhelpful structures, even if those attempts remain imperfect, and a work in progress. But if, on the other hand, your church has never attempted to change anything for as long as you remember, someone may tell you that your church may be a *museum*. Take Oldbury Community Temple, for example—a congregation, founded during the last years of the eighteenth century, with a storied and rich history. Oldbury's early member roll reads like a list of who's who in Oldbury; Oldbury Temple's involvement in the development of the city, Oldbury City Council, and the entire state, is in history books everywhere. When people looked for a church for gentry and respectability, they sought Oldbury, for its city, state, and national prominence.

When Nelson Stollmeyer became Oldbury's sixteenth pastor, he was regarded as young, bright, promising, and timely. He was welcomed by both the congregation and the city; in fact, the city embraced Stollmeyer as their informal chaplain, and many civic entities which required some kind of religious blessing came to Stollmeyer and Oldbury for some form of inclusion in their weekend services.

About four years into his pastorate, Stollmeyer thought it was time to tackle some of the matters he had noticed from the beginning of his tenure—things he considered real and present threats to Oldbury's sustainability. Oldbury had a decent membership and Sunday attendance, and the finances were reasonably satisfactory; so no, those were not the problems. Oldbury's non-ordained leaders, largely, were the challenge. Stollmeyer found that the majority of Oldbury's deacons and other leaders had ascended to their positions more for the prominence they held in the city's government and institutions, or for their education, or more for their favor with persons already serving as deacons, and less—if at all—for their spiritual suitability for the positions. Out of thirty-five deacons and leaders, Stollmeyer could find no more than five whom he had seen in the past four years at the church's midweek Bible Study. Few took advantage of the church's discipleship and Christian education offerings, or the prayer meeting opportunities. Oldbury's deacons had the notion that their ministry existed apart from the pastoral ministry; that it was independent of, and unaccountable to, the pastor, and was completely autonomous; this, in a church with a theology, polity, and governance in which the congregational form of government is usual, expected, and paramount.

The deacons' board had, over the years, denuded the congregation of its right to choose its deacons, and Stollmeyer sought to reverse that. He had seen the very sad spectacle of nominees, both from himself and from the congregation, scoffed at and ridiculed; Stollmeyer watched in dismay while suitable nominees were derided and flippantly dismissed as the deacons sat in conference to do the supposedly prayerful and spiritual work of choosing leaders, even though it was a task they arrogated to themselves, to the congregation's exclusion. Stollmeyer had had enough, and as he taught from the biblical sources what the caliber and qualifications of deacons were expected to be and how they were to be chosen, the forces marshaled themselves against him. These ugly forces manifested themselves in several episodes of pettiness, including even restrictions about how Mrs. Stollmeyer should arrange the furniture in the parsonage. It even included expressions that permission—not merely *information*—should be sought by Pastor Stollmeyer from the deacons before Stollmeyer accepted invitations from other churches, within Oldbury's own denominational family, to minister, speak, or preach! The deacons harassed him about the length of his sermons and sometimes the length of his invitations to salvation, discipleship and membership following sermons. It did not matter that Stollmeyer had become, in the city, state, and denomination, a preacher and teacher in demand. It did not matter that, during his tenure, Oldbury's membership—nearly entirely by baptism—increased by 30 percent in his first four years.

The deacons' concentration and limitation of power within their own ranks marginalized and kept the very vibrant, active, talented, and numerous young adult demographic at Oldbury at bay and in their place. Stollmeyer and his wife worked closely and tirelessly with the youth and young adults. His frequent referral of some of them to the deacons as ready and capable to share in leadership always fell on deaf ears.

The deacons and leaders' harassment, disrespect, and other shenanigans went on for about two years, taking a toll on Stollmeyer—resulting, eventually, in his resignation, after more than six years of faithful and promising leadership. In fact, it was the deacons' entertaining the application of a pastoral candidate while Stollmeyer was *still* Oldbury's pastor, that constituted the final straw on the proverbial camel's back. At the time of Stollmeyer's departure, Oldbury's Sunday attendance at its two morning services (one of which was one of the few things Stollmeyer was able to institute despite the deacons' skepticism and protest) averaged 800 each. The midweek Bible Study and prayer meeting averaged 110.

Within a few months after Stollmeyer's departure, Oldbury's new pastor took his place. He enjoyed better relations with the deacons; however, because it was through non-challenging, non-corrective, and "smooching" relationships, he did not address their abuse of power. He did no leadership development training. His sermons were considered beneath the standard that Stollmeyer, and Stollmeyer's predecessors, set and left. He slowly abandoned the midweek Bible Study, consigning it to a couple of the same deacons and leaders whom Stollmeyer had never seen in Sunday school or Bible Study during his years there. Promising young adults gradually left Oldbury, either falling away among the so-called non-churched, or taking membership in other churches. The youth and children, as they grew up, followed suit.

About two decades after leaving Oldbury, bad weather caused a weekend flight connection to ground Stollmeyer in an airport near the town. He decided to take the opportunity to visit the church. His successor was out of town, but a visiting preacher was in the pulpit. Stollmeyer decided to spend some time spanning both services, so as to greet old friends who happened to be present. He had heard that things had declined at the church, but he was not quite prepared for what he saw: sparse attendance, and an absence of energy in the worship. What used to be eight hundred to a thousand in attendance was—that Sunday (and usual, as he heard)—about one hundred twenty. He learned that midweek services were now defunct. He was shown the vestry where his photograph (of a much younger face and frame) adorned the hallway along with all of Oldbury's pastoral servants before him and the one after. He looked around the sanctuary with all the memorials plaques and stones laid in memory of persons, some dead for nearly two hundred years. He heard about many baptisms that Oldbury continued to have but with no concomitant or evident increase in Sunday morning or midweek attendance, or in useful, developed disciples or leaders. At that very moment, Nelson Stollmeyer recognized that Oldbury Community Temple was no longer a church, but had become a museum. Oldbury—not unlike the Louvre or the Smithsonian—now bore, within pristine and historic architectural environs, the artifacts and memories of the distant past, rather than any effervescent life of the present.

Because Oldbury's leadership had resolutely refused to adopt the best practices of leadership involving shared power, empowerment of all, and the engagement of all at the table, the organization atrophied, yielding a museum rather than a church. What Stollmeyer noticed that Oldbury's leaders considered important during his tenure—against which he fought and lost, and which found full flourish after his departure—were symbols, rather than reality. The Oldbury Community Temple had now become Oldbury Museum.

Chapter 2

The Congregation: One Organization, Four Perspectives

EACH OF THESE FOUR churches to whom you have just been introduced—City Edge Church (the exclusive social club), Ocean View Fellowship (the kingdom), Portland Hill Chapel (the bureaucracy), and Oldbury Community Temple (the Museum)—became this way because of their flawed theology and understanding of ministry; but more than that, they became this way because of how they were organized. Each depicts, respectively, each of the four frames through which organizations can be understood and identified. And each, with an understanding of who they have become organizationally, can (with adjustments ranging from minor to major) become healthy churches.

When Lee Bolman and Terrence Deal got together to write the first edition of their best-seller, *Reframing Organizations,* they could not imagine that a young pastor far across the oceans in a different world and culture, and only in his first year of his first pastorate, would later become a leadership studies student in America, and read their book with the lenses and orientation of congregational and denominational organizations. Since Bolman and Deal's publication, the American church in particular, and global church in general, have seen a slew of significant developmental challenges, much of which stem from organizational dynamics related to these four frames. Included among these congregational and denominational challenges are the following:

(a) Declining attendance and membership;
(b) "Tithes" that are no longer 10 percent, as well as a reduction in other forms of giving;

13

 (c) Falling interest in spiritual development (such as prayer meeting attendance, or even the absence of such an opportunity in many churches);

 (d) Declining enrollment in Christian Education opportunities (for both children and adults);

 (e) Declining credibility in society of both churches and clergy;

 (f) Decline in seminary enrollment along with rising seminary education costs;

 (g) Rising median age of members;

 (h) Rising cynicism and skepticism especially among non-church goers;

 (i) Rising maintenance costs for aging facilities (or inability to continue maintaining them);

 (j) Cutbacks on congregational and denominational staff and employment.

Many of these realities are either due to, or reflective of, organizational dynamics or leadership issues, which are the concerns of this book.

It is these congregational and denominational concerns—as organizations—that Bolman and Deal help us process and understand. They name four organizational frames: the human resource, political, structural, and symbolic.[1] They define a frame as "a mental model—a set of ideas and assumptions—that you carry in your head to help you understand and negotiate a particular 'territory.'"[2] Many of the foregoing issues that challenge the vitality and freshness of the church are due primarily to the church's failure to reinterpret and reassess her mission and role in her present context. One reason the church may be facing these many difficulties and challenges has to do with how the church views itself. On the one hand, some churches resolutely refuse to consider themselves organizations. Such churches are uncomfortable with the idea that, under the definition of organization, the church takes on the character of "worldly" businesses or secular organizations or might benefit from "sinful" principles that govern businesses and other secular organizations. On the other hand, many people are rejecting what they call organized religion, even while many churches do not consider themselves to be organized in the way that businesses and corporations are organized. Of course, a congregation's being organized is not necessarily

1. Bolman and Deal, *Reframing Organizations*, 14.
2. Ibid., 11.

the same as being involved in organized religion. Some congregations, by their independence and non-denominational alignments, might be able to make the claim that they do not belong to organized religion; but then, the term may not mean the same thing to everyone who uses it.

Sometime during the winter of 2016, a religious radio announcer—a priest, on WJMJ, Hartford, Connecticut—was heard lamenting this excuse that many offer for disliking the church: that church is organized religion. He said that he loves a good game of golf; the rules are there, governing the game, managing the players and the movement through the holes. He observed that many of his golfing friends are among those who say they dislike church because it is organized religion. But the priest realized that golf, because of its rules and structure, and the necessity of these rules and structure to ensure a fair, orderly and sensible game, was *organized!* So he concluded that his golfing partners who loved golf, but who said they were against organized religion, were not against organization *per se*, but perhaps were really against religion! Of course, for many, golf (or whatever it is they practice faithfully and frequently) *is* a religion! One might argue, then, that it might be that people are not against religion, but are unhappy with the *way* in which religion, congregations, and denominations are organized! This book takes that position.

In some quarters, congregations are spiritualized as organisms—that is, living bodies, rather than (or more than) ordinary human organizations. It should not be denied that congregations are organisms. That is a theologically sound position. It is also an obvious fact, because congregations comprise people—living people, who cooperate together in their natural lives, and who are also spiritually energized by the living Holy Spirit. But we make the case here that healthy congregations should also make peace with themselves that they *are* organizations. Perhaps one reason churches—compared to businesses, other non-profit, for-profit, and secular organizations—often perform badly and turn out to be exclusive social clubs, kingdoms, bureaucracies, and museums is that, in denying that the church is a business (which it should not be, in a commercial sense), the deniers also tacitly conclude that the church is not an organization. This is a mistake. Congregations should joyfully celebrate their organizational nature as much as they do their spiritual nature. Accepting that they are organizations—and sophisticated ones in some cases—provides touchstones for renewing ministry, missional health, and effectiveness. Bolman and Deal's groundbreaking study of organizations offers some realities about congregations, including your church, from which parishioners, congregational and denominational leaders, and students of congregations and denominations may benefit. All of the congregations we visited in the last chapter demonstrate some disturbing realities, not just about churches, but about organizations in general. Indeed, Bolman and Deal describe organizations as complex, surprising, deceptive, and ambiguous[3]—realities which the reader, no doubt, may have noted. The truths in this assertion shall be in evidence, time and again, in the remainder of this book. Church people, church institutions, and their organizations, which do not desire to be led into dysfunction, should seek deep understanding of themselves through each of Bolman and Deal's organizational frames. They should examine the particular challenges, as well as opportunities for leaders and people and their organizations within each particular frame; and they should know the requirements for effective leadership, as well as the indicators of leadership effectiveness in each frame. All this shall go a very long way to healthy congregations, healthy church organizations, healthy denominational structures, and effective leaders and leadership.

3. Ibid., 31–33.

Chapter 3

Your Church Is A Human Resource Entity

ORGANIZATIONAL DYNAMICS TELL US that your church is a human resource entity. Your church comprises people, and is, in fact, a gathering of (called out) people. Biblically, the church's people are seen as the building blocks of the church;[1] and, as Christ's body, they are understood, metaphorically, to be his body parts.[2] Every builder knows that, from the blueprint to the finished edifice, organization is crucial. Every physician knows—whether it is the lymphatic system or nervous system or skeletal system—that the body is proof of a series of "fearfully and wonderfully"[3] *organized* systems. If it is easy to see organization in the human body, and organization in the human and spiritual body of people called the church, then it should not be difficult to include a human resource perspective when considering the nature of a congregation. To ignore this and to focus only on the spiritual, is to naively devalue and overlook some crucial realities that the church needs, to be as healthy and efficient as it should be. Congregations are human resource entities.

Human resource discipline and perspectives affirm that people are of paramount importance. An organization's people should exceed, in priority of importance, the organization's programs and goals. People are not there just to take orders; neither are they workers merely to be rewarded accordingly, end of story. They carry feelings, possess ideas, have a valid

1. 1 Pet 2:5. Except where otherwise indicated, the New International Version (NIV) is the version quoted in this book.

2. 2 Corinthians 12:27.

3. Ps 139:14.

stake in the organization's well-being, and shape the organization's character, vision, direction, and mission. Organizations that overlook, underrate, undermine, or forget this fact pay a heavy price for it. This is what happened to City Edge Church: they were not merely a social club; they were an *exclusive* social club, in which the only people considered important were the deacons, and only to themselves. They closed ranks on Pastor Hughes, excluded the opinions of the members and actually denied entry to new members! City Edge was a social club with membership for only the deacons and a few other favored ones. As a club, it excluded those who were not members; and to be valued as members, apparently, one had to be a deacon. Ordinarily, a social club might suggest that people are, in fact, important; but in City Edge's case, this was not so. City Edge had been led into dysfunction. And it was the members of their exclusive social club—the exclusive breed of deacons—who led City Edge there. City Edge's deacons cared not for the feelings of their members or even their own new pastor. City Edge's deacons cared, neither for the resourcefulness that reposed in the fledgling church's members, nor for the gifts that their new pastor brought. They were oblivious to the reality that adding new members who, in one fell swoop, would increase the church's membership by 80 percent, would make a monumentally positive impact on the church's mission and ministry. The social club character killed the potential of its human capital and its human resources.

Not every church that falters with its human resources looks like City Edge. There are eight areas against which your church's commitment to being a healthy human resource entity might be tested. Each measurement is introduced by a separate question.

1. *Attrition*: What is the attrition rate, or turnover, experienced in your church's membership, and what does it signify? If people are leaving your church, it may be the first sign that something might be amiss with the value the church places on its human capital. Disappearing church members hardly ever forewarn the rest of us that they are leaving or why; but their departure may often be a call for examining the value and worth members feel they have in the church body, or understand they ought to place in the others in the body.

   Drew Romney and Tommy Traylor were members of Johnsonville Faith Community. Both men were, in fact, respected and valued leaders. With the church's resources underwriting it, Romney had attended several training and development seminars over his many years of membership at Johnsonville; and now, he was a mere three months away from retirement from his job at one of the city's prestigious companies. Romney had promised, for years, that as soon as he retired, he would offer much more of himself to the congregation. But one Sunday, Romney suddenly left the church in annoyance, but not before berating the pastor and some other key leaders in an email, expressing disagreement with the church's attempts to strengthen its relationship with the association of churches which it considered its family. Unfortunately, like so many church goers, Romney didn't see this relationship as family; he saw it as mere denominationalism. Similarly, Traylor, after several decades at Johnsonville, became disenchanted with the church's relationship with the wider association, and left when the leadership did not share his conviction that it should jump ship and embrace a different denomination. Traylor—like so many church goers—considered "jumping ship" rather than "all hands on deck" to be the appropriate response to perceived weaknesses in the congregation or church family.

For Traylor and Romney, what they valued more was their church's individualism above a higher concept of the church as a member of a family. This latter value appears to be fast eroding both in individual church members and individual congregations. At any rate, the attrition of members demands an investigation into what is really afoot when members leave. It may be reflective of the value that the church places on its people, or conversely, the value each church member places on the other members, their family.

2. *Appreciation*: Are there very clear signs in your church which demonstrate that people are genuinely appreciated? Appreciation cannot be skin deep; it has to be thorough and pervasive, or else it shall be disbelieved. Carter Murray noticed that, even though he was pastor of Johnsonville Faith Community, people would pass him by, without greeting, in the foyer or narthex, and sometimes even in the front part of the church office. It is not that Murray was unknown to these people; after all, the church was a small one, in which everybody knew one another. Besides, certain characteristics of Murray's physique would not allow him to be mistaken for anybody else! Further, some of the persons who passed him by as though he did not exist, were leaders. Even though the church had a special item in weekly worship which allowed one member, each Sunday, to be encouraged with words of appreciation by

others in the congregation and a special prayer, Murray himself, did not feel appreciated. Neither did his family members. In fact, it was Murray himself who initiated this very popular worship item. Yet, one Sunday, when one of Johnsonville's key leaders fulsomely praised the initiative several months after it had been in effect, she thanked "whoever it was that started it"—even though *she* was the *first* person Murray selected for this act of encouragement! These and other such events communicated to Murray that he was neither valued nor appreciated, either for his office or his being. Quite apart from himself, Murray noticed the ravages of individualism at Johnsonville, which produced both a lack of depth of relationships in the church and its accompanying failure of Johnsonville's members to truly value anyone outside of their own immediate family or cliques. Appreciation goes beyond words; instead, it is the depth and sincerity of recognition, which includes the notice and celebration of one by another or others. This was absent from Johnsonville Faith Community; and this was perhaps one reason their attrition rate was high.

3. *Relationships*: What is the nature of relationships shared in your church? Genuine appreciation flows from healthy relationships. During a "Friendship Campaign" at Johnsonville Faith Community, two members marveled at the fact that they had been members for thirty-five years, considered each other friends, and yet, neither had ever invited the other to their homes. While Murray and his family routinely invited church members to their home to share a meal, the gesture was rarely reciprocated and never really caught on among the membership as was intended. Johnsonville's relationships were shallow. Johnsonville may have been a social club; it may have been an exclusive one, not in the sense of admitting only a few (as with City Edge's deacons), but exclusive in the sense that the shallowness of relationships excluded members from truly sharing one another's lives. In a social club, all that is required is one's dues, and perhaps some participation in the club's programs in keeping with one's interests; however, in a social club, mutual and intimate concern for, or participation in members' lives, are no requirements. In a healthy church, though, where the participants are valuable human capital sharing life, they see, recognize, and value one another, and share sincere and caring relationships. This is the measure of intimacy that makes the church not just a human resource entity, but a family. Relationships are not always smooth; they are often challenged

by conflict, and this is commonplace in church organizations. Bolman and Deal would recommend that churches "develop relationships by having individuals confront conflict."[4] Churches that seek to be faithful to biblical practices would know this instinctively, given passages such as Ps 133:1, Gal 6:1–10, and Phlm 4:2.

4. *Roles*: In your church, are roles clarified and then well-divided and well-distributed? Do members know what the church's ministries are? Do they know what their skills, talents, and gifts are? Does the leadership help them to discover these and then deploy them? Do they know that they are needed? Are there efforts to constantly connect members with ministry, and move them out of spectatorship? Often, when churches attempt to do some of this, some of the members, satisfied to be mere social club members, do not respond adequately or meaningfully. In Portland Hill Chapel, when the congregation was attempting to discern a new form of efficiency, a spiritual gifts survey instrument was made available for all of Portland Hill's two hundred members to complete, in order to distribute ministry activity within the new government. Only thirty-three members completed the survey, oblivious to the crucial need for this information and its relevance to the church's new journey. This would, in time, have a deleterious impact on Portland Hill's viability as a healthy church; this contributed also to the church's bureaucracy status. The willingness of only one-sixth of a congregation to participate in such a crucial human resource exercise is indicative of their failure to understand that their church is as much a human resource entity as it is a ministry entity. In congregations, the two are inseparable.

5. *Security*: Do your pastor and other paid staff have a sense of security? In congregations that call their own pastor, there is always a risk of what is known as forced termination. Forced termination is when pressure is applied to a pastor, overtly or covertly, directly or indirectly, in such a way as to cause her or him to be frustrated into resignation, or to be asked to resign, or, in some cases, dismissed from the congregation. Although a pastor or other key staff are not a congregation's *only* human resource capital, they may be a congregation's most pivotal human resources. It should be commonplace that congregations view their pastors as spiritual leaders. But often, that is all they are considered to be. When Pastor Hughes was being harassed by his deacons at City Edge

---

4. Bolman and Deal, *Reframing Organizations*, 314.

Church, one of his supporters defended him before the exclusive club, saying, "But he is our leader!" A very adamant club member retorted, with great indignation, "No! He is our *spiritual* leader!" She was careful to make a distinction between spiritual leadership and the serious human resource leadership that reposes in pastors. It is, of course—and in most congregational contexts—an artificial and fallacious distinction. Hughes's pastoral tenure lasted only a few weeks beyond this incident. It is this failure to understand their pastors as gifts of human capital, that contributed to City Edge's fast and flagrant dismissal of their pastors once every twenty-two months or so during the previous two decades. None of these hapless pastors had the kind of security that is required to communicate that a congregation recognizes that it is a human resource entity, and that that identity is a characteristic of its spiritual identity. We shall visit, in chapter 10, the dilemma that pastors face, in being both employee and leader at the same time, within the same—often small—organization.

6. *Development*: Does your church pay attention to, and invest time and money in, leadership development? Do your church's boards, committees, and ministry teams behave—among other things—as intentional leadership development vehicles? Chances are, if your church still functions with boards and committees and knows nothing about ministry teams, the answer is no. Then too, if your church does function with ministry teams, the answer might still be no. Are persons rotated through ministries or leadership positions, or has the same person been chair of deacons, or church clerk, or moderator, or worship development leader, or Christmas events planner for the last ten, twenty, or thirty years? If the answer is yes, then it is time for a leadership and membership development check-up.

   Human resources thrive on development. Because a church is an organism just like any other living plant, person, reptile, or animal, it needs to grow. Growth also implies necessary development and its facilitation. Bolman and Deal remind us that, in the human resource mode, an organizantion's life should be about "growth and self-actualization."[5] In a church organization, the facilitation of the members' development is just as crucial. The best human resource practices call for constant human capital development, whether in the

5. Ibid., 315.

various forms of continuing education, or in-house retreats, or other forms of training.

Some churches' board or council meetings are a very dry experience. The participants gather, pray a perfunctory prayer, and jump right in to business, and are done within an hour or two, or perhaps three, if there are arguments and fights. Apart from a careful exercise of reflection on biblical scripture, other churches include reflection and discussion on a paper, article, or book regarding trends in ministry, leadership, and human engagement. These are geared to sharpen church leaders' appreciation of the present, and develop vision for the future. There are many such resources available to churches today, whether through their denominations, or in magazines and periodicals and the Internet. In colleges and universities, service learning has now become commonplace. Higher education administrators know the power of this form of development alongside the students' academic performance and growth. Churches may need to understand ministry and church life as service learning; even Jesus—the one who called disciples (students) to follow him and serve—would agree! A church in which *all* of its leaders are not participating in some form of continuing education, or in which *all* of its members are not being encouraged to view themselves as being in training for ministry and possibly leadership, may be a church that is being led into dysfunction, slowly, but surely.

7. *Support*: What is the level of support given to members and to leaders in your church? Are people elected to positions of service and leadership, and thereafter abandoned or otherwise left starving for support from the very people that elected them? Do people in your church make expressions of encouragement to the persons who serve and lead them? Is there a culture of inquiry about the well-being of one another? Are people willing to join ministry teams, or give money to support the church's ministry? Do they look for opportunities to celebrate (not only their own events or their family's)? Is the biblical expectation true of your church: that when one rejoices, all rejoice, and when one suffers, all suffer?[6] Is there a culture of creativity and recreating, and designing and redesigning ministry and the organization itself, so that the best gifts of the people may have space to be happily utilized and the people themselves have opportunity to flourish?

6. 1 Cor 12:26.

And what about criticisms and correction: are they done without injury to others and with the genuine warmth and assurance of care and true love? Bolman and Deal observe that, in the matter of evaluating an organization's progress, "feedback [is] for helping individuals grow and improve."[7]

8. *Autonomy and Accountability*: What level of autonomy do members have to dream visions of ministry, to create the framework for that ministry, and to complete the ministry? How much initiative are they allowed to exercise? Where human capital is valued, autonomy and initiative would be at a high level, in which church leaders and members would feel free to be creative and adventurous. This amounts to empowerment—a condition in which, among other things, the "least" of the members are made to feel as responsible for the development of the work as do the chief of the leaders. They share the power of initiative; and where this power is shared, much more is likely to be accomplished by the organization, provided there is a guiding, overarching, single, and shared vision, known to all. Of course, conventional organizational wisdom suggests that where the levels of autonomy and initiative are high, the level of accountability should be commensurately high.

Cheryl Grier was a stickler for developing young adult leadership in her church. She encouraged the ministry leaders to develop and chart their own course in the ministries they led. As pastor, Grier reserved the right to sign off on the shape of each Sunday's worship, seeing that she understood her pastoral role as worship leader, even if others led the worship events on Sundays. Further, she reserved the right to make any changes or adjustments that the worship team developed. Nevertheless, that was a right that Grier rarely exercised. Sometimes she would enable the ministry leader for worship, as well as the music director, to see a theological perspective that only Grier's trained and pastoral eye would catch, and they would make adjustments. Conversely, sometimes those leaders would raise their perspectives with Grier, and she would make adjustments to the morning's worship sequence and contents in accordance with their perspectives.

There came a time, though, when one of the leaders was not prepared to make an adjustment to the worship order after Grier signed off on it. Rather than exercising the accountability that would require humble cooperation with the rule that Grier and her leaders had exercised

7. Bolman and Deal, *Reframing Organizations*, 314.

for years, one ministry leader complained to a powerful leader. That leader inveigled his all-male colleagues to use this opportunity to declare Grier's leadership as ineffective, and require her resignation. The leaders had never before, in all of Grier's years in that congregation, so adjudged her leadership. Grier viewed this as a dysfunctional abuse of autonomy and initiative. Apart from feeling that her seven years of service were as unrecognized as she was, Grier felt that the proverbial dog had just bit her hand, which fed it, in that, the very leaders she empowered, trained, and gave adequate leeway to discharge their gifts and ministry, turned around and destroyed her.

Churches whose human resources receive the gift of autonomy and initiative for doing ministry are destined for dysfunction, should they circumvent any lines of accountability expected of them.

When one accepts Bolman and Deal's human resource frame as applicable to church organizations, one would hold the following as true about congregations and denominations: (a) their "gatherings [are] to promote participation";[8] and are "informal occasions for involvement [and] sharing feelings";[9] (b) they seek an "open process to produce commitment";[10] and (c) they "maintain a balance between human needs and formal roles."[11] Churches are human resource entities; they are places where all should be valued, where the diversity of human gifts and differences should be celebrated in unity and in harmony, and where a generous egalitarianism should prevail, rendering in each church a holistic body and a joyful family.

believing in the principle that all people are equal and deserve equal rights and opportunities

---

8. Ibid.
9. Ibid., 315.
10. Ibid., 314.
11. Ibid.

Chapter 4

Your Church Is A Political Entity

IN CONGREGATIONAL AND DENOMINATIONAL life, and among the people who comprise the church, we should be full of the Spirit and *moved* by the same Spirit; however, an onlooker may differ, concluding that too often, we are moved, more by the desires, designs, and machinations of human power and power plays, than by the Spirit. Unfortunately, these power plays, in church and denomination, are frequently of a nature that might make even the Mafia blush.

DEMONSTRATIONS OF CONGREGATIONAL AND DENOMINATIONAL POWER.

The late Wilmot Perkins, a prominent Jamaican journalist, with prowess in the print media and, later, perhaps Jamaica's best-loved, highest-rated, most controversial, and longest-running talk show host, wrote an article in the *Jamaica Gleaner* back in the early 1980s. He began by saying that the church is the author of totalitarianism. As disturbing or even offensive as this statement might be to some church members, anyone with a knowledge of history, as well as wide experience in congregational life, may come to sympathize with that statement. Perkins himself was once a seminarian, preparing for the Christian ministry. He did not complete that journey, but instead became a journalist who served Jamaica very well, and was a constant thorn in the flesh of politicians who behaved badly. This, added to his very wide and almost encyclopedic range of reading and knowledge, as well as his intimidating intellect, should assure even one who might disagree, that Perkins knew what he was talking about—both about bad politics and badly utilized power in churches.

Priscilla Young was a young pastor in the Airedale Convention of Churches. She had prepared a paper for the annual pastors and leaders' conference, in which she listed some observations and concerns about the convention's trajectory in leadership development. Young was once an executive member of a smaller convention for seven years, and had served, too, as the president of that convention. In the larger Airedale Convention, Young observed and lamented among other things, the following: (a) a lack of intentional leadership development, (b) elitism in selecting and granting opportunities for development and ascension to certain offices, (c) a helter-skelter, free-for-all format of continuing education for pastors that did not serve the convention well, and (d) the convention's disdainful disinterest in the affairs of its wider regional denominational family.

Before Young could get barely ten minutes into her presentation, a senior pastor, joined by a chorus of other senior and powerful pastors, objected to her comments. The room, with nearly a hundred other pastors present, sat in silence. All of Young's colleagues sat in stony silence; none rose to her defense, including the moderator of the event—the convention's president. Although Young had secured the president's permission to present her paper, the president, upon seeing the hot conflagration surrounding Young (and no doubt not wanting to accept any responsibility for facilitating Young), flatly denied having given her the clearance to present her paper. Young was angrily silenced, vehemently criticized, and made to sit down in humiliation, never having the opportunity to flesh out either what she was offering as concerns (but which were unfortunately received as negative criticisms) or the strategies she would suggest. She did not get beyond page one.

In ensuing years, at the convention's annual meetings, Young would chuckle to herself as reports from key operatives would lament some of the very issues she would have raised in her paper. Twenty-five years after Young's defeat, the Airedale Convention of Churches has a massive leadership crisis: its membership is stagnant (on paper, that is, but declined in reality), its finances are tenuous, and its pastoral staff performance is generally dissatisfactory, reflecting ministerial standards that are of grave concern. There is also a significant and acute dearth of persons adequately groomed, trained or exposed to the ways of the convention's "inner circle," so as to seamlessly merge into key leadership positions. These positions, always understood elsewhere as vital for denominational and congregational life, were considered by some in the Airedale Convention, during the time when Young's presentation was thrown out, as prizes for special people. Now, years later, Airedale is in trouble, because it possesses an inadequate number of persons who have been prepared either directly or tangentially, for key leadership positions.

Twenty-five years later, Young's fierce objectors have either died or retired. The vast majority of her colleagues, intimidated into impotent silence that day, have now matured into—one might reasonably guess— a *very* silent and impotent ministry team; and only a sliver of a fraction of them have become the kind of leaders that the convention needs. Even among that fraction are prevailing, palpable, and pervasive attitudes of entitlement, officiousness, and superiority, rather than collegiality, which comprise a trinity of deterrents to the spirit of partnership, encouragement, growth, harmony, peace, and joy. Many of the convention's pastors, having embarked on a ministry that breeds this culture, have themselves become—despite whatever potential they may have brought to the table—just like the others they met; for an organism reproduces after its own kind. Unfortunately, organizations, without adequate intervention, do the same. The Airedale Convention of Churches has been led toward dysfunction, on a journey which is almost complete. That convention is a picture of politics at work, in an unhealthy way.

Politics is at work in every human organization, including the church, and it may be at work in healthy ways as well as in unhealthy ways. In her earlier years of ministry, Priscilla Young frequently said of herself, "I am a pastor, not a politician." That was Young's first mistake. Had she understood some of the dynamics of politics, or understood that churches are fraught with as much of the unhealthy displays of politics as well as blessed with the opportunities to exercise the healthy forms, she might have navigated her fateful pastors' conference better, and with a measure of success. Had she understood herself through political lenses and operated as such, she might have managed her career better, earlier. Had she considered the accusation that "the church is the author of totalitarianism" or had she reached the conclusion, far earlier than she did in her middle years of ministry, that the church is the father of all politics (not *mother* as she thought in an earlier iteration of her philosophy), the pastors conference, twenty-five years earlier, might have had a different ending. Says Bolman and Deal, "The question is not whether organizations are political but what kind of politics they will encompass."[1]

---

1. Bolman and Deal, *Reframing Organizations*, 228.

When Glenroy Hughes was dismissed from City Edge Church—the exclusive social club—it was a raw display of even more raw and unbridled power that took him down. Although the church's bylaws required that a pastor's dismissal be by congregational vote in a specially called meeting, Hughes's dismissal was not on these terms. The deacons, after destroying the worship service, boycotted a legitimately called congregational meeting, convened after the service. They refused to cooperate with the directives offered by Conrad, the denominational representative. Conrad had been the church's trusted and competent consultant and guide through many years and many messes that the deacons had created. Conrad shuttled back and forth between the congregational meeting that Hughes chaired—a meeting, properly called to express a lack of confidence in the deacons and some other leaders' stewardship—and the renegade deacons' kangaroo court of a meeting. He reported to Hughes and the fledgling group of parishioners that he kept warning the deacons that their meeting was unconstitutional and that the meeting Hughes was chairing was legitimate. Nevertheless, the deacons, church secretary and church moderator, all of whom held the keys to the building, and all the instruments of power, secured the services of a lawyer who issued the letter to Hughes six days later, informing him of his dismissal. Even though Hughes had grounds to fight this decision legally (and had begun exploring them), he hadn't the energy or funds to continue. This was compounded by his discovery that the legal fraternity in his state were hesitant about pursuing ecclesiastical matters in court. So the City Edge deacons, secretary, and moderator won. It was a pyrrhic victory, though, because with Hughes departure, the Sunday attendance at City Edge shrank, permanently, to less than ten. The only thing that kept City Edge's doors open was the poor stewardship of the church's endowment, managed by a treasurer who had not made her appearance at City Edge for over three decades! In time to come, that endowment was depleted. City Edge's dozen members' financial giving was no match for the maintenance-hungry, hundred-and-ten-year-old aging facilities and buildings. Even though City Edge has not yet closed, its life and ministry has, by many measurements, long since ended. Power—the concentrated remit of a few, and employed to abuse many—has led City Edge not merely to dysfunction, but has placed it on the road to extinction.

SOURCES OF CONGREGATIONAL AND
DENOMINATIONAL POWER

The foregoing demonstrations of power are, of course, the unhealthy kind. The sources of power for congregations and denominations indicate, though, that such power is good and meant to be exercised for good. They indicate that politics in church organizations is meant to be about shared power and a distribution of power that is meant to heal, build, engage, and unify, rather than to repel, abuse, intimidate, or—to use the word of the church's founder—"lord" it over anyone.[2]

Gill identifies different kinds of power, categorizing them into *authority* (or position) power and *personal* power.[3] Among the former is legitimate power, "based on people's perception of the . . . leader's right or authority to make them do something because of his or her role or position in the organization."[4] Among the primary sources of power in church organizations is ordination. Regardless of the tradition within which ordination is practiced, and regardless of the complexity of its concept, ordination is considered to be the conferral of power. Because the understanding is that the source of that power is God, that power is considered holy power. However, it is power that is also meant to lead God's people, discharge God's order, and enable the church's execution of God's will in the world. Halliburton appears to support this assertion. He notes that "positions of responsibility and leadership in the early Christian communities were not filled simply by election, but those holding them required authorization or commission."[5] Despite Gill's definition of legitimate power, ordination power is not understood by many ordained persons as the authority to "make people do something" as much as it is understood as spiritual authority that *invites* people to share in discovering and engaging in God's will and work. Ordination is either the route through which ministers ascend to leadership, and the exercise of power, or the affirmation of their suitability to use holy (and other kinds of) power responsibly. When this conferral of power is done upon the right person, it is supportive of the congregation or denomination's good order. When this is done, it enables the right discovery and distribution of energies, gifts, talents, skills, and

2. Matt 20:25; 1 Pet 5:2–3.

3. Gill, *Theory*, 267.

4. Ibid., 266–67.

5. Halliburton, *Authority*, 78.

ministry, all of which repose in the people who comprise the congregation or religious entity. This is not ordinarily considered politics, but it is, in fact. It is just not *partisan* or *secular* politics.

Within the category of personal power, Gill identifies *expert* power and *information* power.[6] Both related, it would appear that, in congregational and denominational organizations, these kinds of power emanate from the leaders' and members' knowledge of their scriptures, constitutions and by-laws, policies, and current magazines, materials, and resources that address ministry, theological, organizational, and leadership issues. But knowledge can certainly be feigned; and the possession of *special,* or *classified,* or *spiritual* knowledge can be not only feigned, but also exaggerated. When this happens, power is corrupted and politics become dirty. A church leader (or member) may claim special spiritual knowledge, either because they really think they do possess it, or pretend to. When these claims go unchecked or uncorrected by the rest of the faith community, the claimant uses this to control the whole community, or other individuals therein.

Expert power—the competence, drawn from the leader's knowledge and information as well as training and experience—is "based on others' perception of a leader's competence, skills, or expertise."[7] This power encourages people to respond favorably and positively to the leader's influence. There is a danger, as Gill notes: that "leaders who display a powerful 'leader demeanor' may boost their appearance of competence (and) also stifle contributions by followers or subordinates."[8]

Expert power is not the only power or source thereof in church organizations, that might be exaggerated, or otherwise corrupted. Consider what Gill calls *referent* power: "the influence that leaders can exert as a result of their perceived attractiveness, personal characteristics or social skills (e.g., charm), reputation or charisma in the eyes of the followers."[9] There remains evidence of this power having been abused in religious organizations, whether it was Jim Jones in the tragedy of the Guyana massacre, David Koresh of the Branch Davidians in Waco, Texas, or Warren Jeffs of the Fundamentalist Latter Day Saints organization in Utah. In between, characters like the charming Terry Fellowes, the "king" of Ocean View Fellowship (the "kingdom"), emerge in congregational and denominational

6. Gill, *Theory,* 267.

7. Ibid., 269.

8. Ibid.

9. Ibid., 268.

life and organizations, even if with less devastating consequences than spawned by the likes of Jeffs, Koresh and Jones.

Other sources of power, and areas where both a healthy use or abuse of power in congregations and denominations can be seen, include financial contributions, longevity, social status, the gift of gab, and more. Persons can use financial gifts to offer power to the church organization, as well as wield it or withhold it so as to use that power for personal gain. Similarly, longevity, social standing, and communication skills can all be leveraged for the sound development of the church organization, as well as be manipulated for creating personal power or cliques or other unhealthy power bases that can damage or destroy the organization's health. All of this use and abuse of power demonstrates clearly that churches and denominational organizations are political entities.

RESPONSES TO THE ABUSE OF CONGREGATIONAL POWER

When power is misused, abused, manipulated, or leveraged for uses other than the harmonious development of the congregation, the denomination, or other religious organization, it is certain to create conflict. Indeed, conflict is likely to be the first, and most pervasive and persistent, outcome of the abuse of power, and bad politics. So what is a congregation to do when this happens? There are three steps that answer this question, the first of which is to be taken *before* conflict arises (the other two, after it does): mitigating conflict, navigating conflict, and interrogating conflict.

Mitigating conflict

Conflict cannot always be prevented; indeed, some conflict is helpful to organizations, alerting its members to discomforts and giving reality checks that can ward off complacency. Not all conflict is good, as everyone knows. Congregations can mitigate conflict in several ways, including the following:

(a) They can ensure that leaders are chosen properly and purposefully, and that such leaders are able and willing, and subscribe to the best values of the congregation;

(b) They can ensure that expectations of both leaders and members are clearly (and perhaps regularly) articulated and reaffirmed;

(c) They can renew their relationships not merely as members of an organization, but as people of a divine covenant;

(d)   They should devise a behavioral covenant that governs how they would behave and conduct themselves when conflict arises; and

(e)   They should consider setting high standards for membership and leadership. Low standards or no standards can easily foment improper and unhealthy behavior and the abuse of power.

Navigating conflict

This is perhaps the most extensive of the three steps. Even in congregations, one of their foremost requirements is that their leaders be disabused of the idea that they would be successful pastors, bishops or other designations, without some measure of political savvy. This was Priscilla Young's primary mistake in the Airedale Convention of Churches. Leaders who hope to intervene in any way with organizational adjustment or transformation need political skills. They cannot rely only on the "goodness of God" if that is understood as being devoid of knowing the ways of humans. Even the great Moses desperately needed the political skills he learned from his father-in-law,[10] and Solomon appeared to be generously outfitted with it, in the form of his legendary wisdom. Congregational leaders, especially pastors, should learn political skills. Seminaries should either teach these skills or require academic credits in politics as a prerequisite for graduation; and denominations should encourage, if not require, their candidates for ordination to be *au fait* with the rudiments of organizational politics.

Some of the indispensable skills, identified by Bolman and Deal and required by pastors for effective congregational leadership, are neither learned nor intentionally taught in seminary. These include agenda setting, mapping the political terrain, networking and building coalitions, bargaining and negotiation.[11] Agenda setting in this context is, of course, less about the ordering of meetings and more about charting the church organization's course, determining what its focus shall be, and what would consume its energies, attention, and time.

The matter of negotiation and bargaining raises the question of conflict management, resolution, and transformation. Every pastor and every congregational leader should have some measure of exposure or education

---

10. See Exodus 18.

11. Bolman and Deal, *Reframing Organizations*, 214–24.

in this skill, because congregations are notorious for generating conflict, and many are just as notorious for inadequately navigating conflict. The attrition rate of pastors, either from the ministry altogether, or by forced terminations or unhappy resignations, is adequate evidence of this. The church-shopping that people do is partly indicative of this fact. The many persons who no longer attend church or identify with any Christian denomination (but used to) betrays, in part, the prevalence of conflict in congregational life. Churches without leaders adequately prepared to tackle this consistent and ever-present problem are being led into dysfunction.

In congregations, both leaders and members would be well-served if they equipped themselves with skills to counter behaviors and attitudes that constitute threats to the harmony, ethos, and development of the organization. The error of some congregations is to consider the scriptures alone as adequate for tackling these challenges. Indeed, the scriptures are considered by many as adequate for matters of faith and practice; however, sociological, political, and organizational concerns are neither the primary nor intended focus of the Bible. So, congregations and denominational agencies would be wise to consult with these disciplines to address the political issues (people issues) that attend their organizations. In congregations, strategy should not be considered inferior to scriptures or as the scriptures' adversary. Congregations already consider scriptural and spiritual suasion as importantly as they consider moral suasion (and in many cases there is no discernible seam between the three); so adding political savvy to pastoral, congregational, and denominational strategy is a wise option. Often, religion goes bad, not because the scriptures are defective; it goes bad because of the abuse of power, especially where there is a poverty of political savvy and strategy among both leaders and members to enable them to happily navigate conflict and ward off dysfunction.

One of the elements of effective conflict management (which itself is an element of effective organizational management) is the idea of win-win.[12] The idiom "there will be winners and losers" may apply to a sporting match or an electoral contest; but in organizations where there is meant to be meaningful and harmonious relationships, the leaders and members need to debunk that idea and pursue, as hard as possible, a win-win situation in as many cases as can be secured. Christian congregations understand themselves as a body—*the* body of Christ,[13] in which unity is

12. Fisher and Ury explore this mechanism in *Getting to Yes.*

13. 1 Cor 12:27.

paramount and required to be jealously maintained.[14] That unity, though not to be misconstrued as uniformity, nevertheless implies an extremely high quality of harmony in which members are urged to "honor one another above yourselves."[15] What these verses—along with the entire ethos of Christian community from which they emanate—indicate is an inherent management of power, a management that enjoins a tempering of the human appetites and attitudes that engender indiscipline and the abuse of power. When this is done, the congregation can better pursue win-win situations together, rejoice together, share mutual benefits, gains, and happy outcomes. Inherent in the scriptures is a call for sharpening people-management skills within the congregation's leadership and membership.

Among the most needful and effective means of navigating conflict is the use of coalitions. Quite often, it is coalitions that have become either toxic or have developed their own agenda that is at variance with the organization's agenda, that cause conflict. This fact is borne out by Bolman and Deal, who "highlight organizations as freewheeling coalitions rather than formal hierarchies. Coalitions are tools for exercising power, and we contrast power with authority and highlight tensions between authorities."[16] While organizations should not be encouraged to fight fire with fire, one way in which toxic, or mischievous, or unruly, or self-serving, leaders can be countered is with coalitions. Bolman and Deal use the metaphor of *jungle* to describe organizations when viewed through the political frame.[17] Persons familiar with congregational conflict might readily, if not sheepishly (pun intended), affirm this description. Lipman-Blumen includes creating coalitions among an organization's arsenal for dealing with the political problem of toxic leaders. She would encourage congregations and denominations to "strategize about how the group will confront the leader and try to structure the confrontation as constructively as possible. If possible, frame your concerns in terms of organizational impact; that is, how the leader's decisions and actions have negatively affected the organization and the people in it."[18] One of the biggest mistakes a congregation can make is for the flock of meek sheep to cower away when the coalition of rams lock their horns in coalition. Not even praying sheep can correct that

14. Eph 4:3.

15. Rom 12:10.

16. Bolman and Deal, *Reframing Organizations*, 194.

17. Ibid., 18.

18. Lipman-Blumen, "Allure," 6.

problem—unless, while in prayer, they heard a divine voice to get up and act in a coalition of spirituality (to which the Apostle Paul seems to allude in Gal 6:1) and acted on that voice in obedience when the prayer was over.

Interrogating conflict

Thirdly, congregations should include *interrogating* conflict in their response to abuses of power. There is much for any organization to learn from their own conflict, if they would only ask the right questions. Congregations and their leaders should sit down and ask themselves:

(a) How did we get to this stage?

(b) What signs did we miss?

(c) Whom did we exclude in the process or issues that led to this current crisis, who should have been around the table, who were excluded?

(d) Whom did we allow to run too far with their own agenda before we unsuccessfully attempted to rein them in, back to the interests of the community?

(e) What does this crisis tell us about our values?

(f) Which of our values have been violated?

(g) What measures can we adopt to prevent a recurrence of this conflict and crisis?

Of course, not all of these questions might be asked in open sessions or even phrased in the frontal way they are outlined here; but they need to be asked by someone, and the answers revealed to many. Interrogating conflict can enable congregations and church organizations to engage in reflection, which is a form of meditation, too little of which even the faithful manage to do. When people reflect together on their common experiences, good or bad, it fosters the kind of unity and community health which all good politics pursues.

In the organization's *jungle* of political realities, conflict, as well as many other pitfalls, would be mitigated, reduced, or even avoided, if church leaders and church people understood their various meetings and fellowship as "arenas to air conflicts and realign power."[19] This power, of course, is not to be understood as the domain of one or a few; but rather it is the

---

19. Ibid., 315.

constant redistribution of power within and among community members. It involves a commitment to breaking up old coalitions that have either served their useful, healthy, and community purpose, or which have gone toxic; followed by the formation of new coalitions which are purposeful and healthy, and serve the community rather than themselves. This constant redistribution of power serves to empower the entire community, rather than just a chosen few.[20] None of this should suggest the absence of persuasion, dialogue, rigorous debate, disagreement, or even bargaining, competition, coercion, seduction, and manipulation[21] during the process of meetings (although, in church circles, there might be a discomfort with the latter three, depending on how they are understood). However, because the commitment is to the sharing of power throughout the entire organization or congregation, that commitment itself should serve to temper the process toward the health of the community rather than to the aggrandizement of one or a few.

20. Ibid.

21. Bolman and Deal envisage bargaining, competition, coercion, seduction, and manipulation as instruments that might be used in organizational processes. See *Reframing Organizations*, 314-15.

Chapter 5

Your Church Is A Structural Entity

IT IS PERFECTLY LOGICAL that anything that either exists or is tangible, or any organization that can be viewed, visited, inspected, or experienced, has structure. It is incorrect to accuse an organization of having no structure, though the sentiment may wish to indicate a lack of *intelligent* or *intentional* structure. In that regard, it is better for congregations to define their structure, rather than their structure defining them! Congregations are better off intentionally forming their structure, than operating haphazardly. In the latter case, structure of the unintended, unintelligible, and unhealthy kind comes to them.

First, the bad news: many congregations do allow structure to come to them. While most congregations may have bylaws and constitutions, are organized for worship, and may have a program or two, many congregations have little beyond that, in terms of structure. Some have no mission statements. Some do, but they are so vague, and so non-action-oriented or non-specific, that they are rendered useless. Some have no vision statement. Many more have no strategic plan. A test, if carried out within the average congregation, asking, "What is your church structured to accomplish?" might be instructive, and might demonstrate how little intentional and intelligent structure some—if not many—congregations possess.

So then, a congregation is a structural entity, whether or not it plans to be. If it intentionally plans to be a structural entity, there would be rhyme and reason, form and fashion to its existence, ministry, and impact. If it does not plan its structure, that structure, having developed a life of its own, would lead the church into confusion, hit-and-miss ministry, inefficiency, ineffectiveness, lack of desired impact on its communities, and in the end, dysfunction.

When a congregation is structurally sound, it is committed to a culture of goal-setting that depicts and demonstrates intentional and intelligent form. The chief organizational culture within that congregation would be setting goals, making plans to reach those goals, and executing those plans, all in accordance with the congregation's robust vision, which would have informed and dictated the goals in the first place. All of the congregation's actions flow from those goals, and toward that vision. This is the picture of a congregation for whom structure is intentional and actionable, rather than accidental. Bolman and Deal identify, as the number one assumption governing organizations in the structural frame, that "organizations exist to achieve established goals and objectives."[1] The good news is that all of this is not only relatively easy to do, though requiring disciplined and patient work, but eminently better than not planning and not intentionally designing the congregation's structure.

The very next assumption Bolman and Deal name as governing the structural frame is that "organizations increase efficiency and enhance performance through specialization and appropriate division of labor."[2] Even though Stephanie Grantley found fifty-five ministries at Portland Hill Church when she arrived there, she observed that not only were the majority of them not functioning, but also that identifying persons to lead ministries was an elusive prospect. Among the measures that Grantley laid out was a spiritual gifts survey, which she invited all of Portland Hill's members to complete. From an active congregation of around two hundred, only thirty-three completed the survey. But even with only one-sixth of the congregation doing so, Grantley and the church council found that the completed survey was signally invaluable. It not only helped the members completing them to discover their own talents, abilities, and gifts some of them never knew they had; above all, it enabled the church's ministry leaders to identify persons who could be recruited for ministry actions, projects and missions, not only at short notice, but in keeping with their interests, talents, skills and gifts. This made a significant difference in the congregation. Even though the Portland Hill Church was functioning beneath its fullest potential, the benefits of their partially completed gifts survey has made a life-giving difference in the congregation. This, because Portland Hill took a couple of significant steps in sorting out its structure: first, its governance, and second, its workforce.

1. Ibid., 47.
2. Ibid.

A church or church organization in the structural mode will be committed to discovering and harnessing all of their gifts, talents, and skills; and they would leverage them for efficiency, for accomplishing their mission, and for fulfilling the purpose of their structure. They do all of this with attention to adequate flexibility and accountability so as to prevent, reduce, and remove "red tape", on the one hand, and atrophy on the other.

The remaining four assumptions that Bolman and Deal identify as essential to the structural perspective of organizations are noteworthy. The first has to do with adequate coordination of the organization's people and initiatives; the second, making sure that "rationality prevails over personal agendas and extraneous pressures";[3] the third, aligning the organization's structure with its "goals, technology, workforce and environment";[4] and the last, that organizations which are willing to do the requisite evaluations and analyses of themselves, as well as restructure themselves, shall surmount performance and other problems, as well as structural flaws.[5]

The first thing that all of this means for congregations is that congregations, which affirm their existence as the body of Christ in which every member is gifted with the gifts, energies, and services of the Spirit,[6] are obligated—when that body is working well—to ensure that "each part does its work."[7] Congregations, whether they are ordered by hierarchical forms of government or not, should ensure that leaders at all levels are engaged in the parity of sisterhood and brotherhood, exchanging ideas, clarifying vision, and discerning the path forward for the congregation. Power of all forms and at every level is to be leveraged, not to outrank or lord it over anyone; instead, power is to be aligned with abilities and partnerships, so as to serve the congregation's best interests, rather than any other narrow personal or sectarian interests. It is essential for congregations to guard against anything that thwarts careful deliberations and conscientious discussions that result in solid discernment regarding the congregation's objectives and goals.

The Airedale Convention of Churches which we visited earlier demonstrates the woes that await a congregation, church organization, or even a denomination, when there is a reluctance, or even refusal, to do the hard work of self-evaluation and the even harder work of recalibrating and

3. Ibid.
4. Ibid.
5. Ibid.
6. 1 Cor 12:4–7.
7. Eph 4:16.

restructuring, required of the analysis and evaluation. Rather than embracing the critical analysis and corrective observation from one of their pastors, Airedale's leaders shut her down, rejected her wisdom as youthful zeal, and misguided folly. They never once considered that there could be value to Priscilla Young's observations. To this day, the Airedale Convention pays the price with several dysfunctional aspects of the denomination's operation. Congregations and church organizations that are impatient of self-evaluation and revision of their ethos, mission, and structure, will all pay a heavy price sooner or later.

The second thing that all of this means is that two fundamental biblical and Christian values—those of highly honoring one another[8] and listening to one another[9]—are always to be upheld in congregational and denominational life. Any observant person long experienced in congregational or denominational life would be able to identify any contrary behaviors in their own contexts. Favoritism has no place in congregational and denominational life. Carol Strang, in her long years in church life, has observed time and again, especially in denominational meetings, value being given to the contributions of some, but not others, whether along lines of age, education, or race. Strang herself, when she was a younger pastor, experienced her comments being ignored, only to hear them mentioned by a senior pastor (sometimes claimed as that person's own idea!) and rousingly welcomed as a novel and wise idea! This is one kind of behavior that is challenged in the advice that "organizations work best when rationality prevails over personal agendas."[10] These attitudes not only devalue and underdevelop people (who are any organization's most valuable asset; the act of underdeveloping them is patently contrary to Christ's way), but they gnaw away at a church organization's very structure. Whenever and wherever they are found, they sound the alarm for a review of organizational structure, perhaps to see whether there are structural flaws in the first place, or whether the organization has strayed from its sound structural premise. That review would remind the organization of what it really values and seeks to achieve. It would recall their understanding of themselves as the body of Christ in which all members are equally important; and it would encourage a reckoning with whether the church organization can ever truly become what it should, or ever become structurally strong, without honoring, developing, and engaging every one of its members.

8. Rom 12:10.

9. 1 Cor 14:29–31.

10. Bolman and Deal, *Reframing Organizations*, 47.

CHALLENGES FOR THE CONGREGATION IN THE STRUCTURAL MODE

Bolman and Deal observe that "most people problems stem from structural flaws, not personal limitation or liability."[11] Surely, what this means is that often, when disquiet, unrest, tensions, and conflict arise in an organization, it is not so much defects in personnel that are to blame; instead, the organization's structure may be the culprit. There is no reason to doubt that this is so when the organization is congregational or denominational. Indeed, Kenneth Jackson, an African-American, became the first man of color to hold the position of pastor of the Riverdale United Church. Under its previous pastors, Riverdale's demographics had changed, resulting in a majority of African immigrants, along with African-Americans, Caribbean immigrants, and Euro-Americans forming the small, smaller, and smallest minorities respectively. Several years after the church made this transition, Riverdale still operated on a structure with which its former majority (the Euro-Americans) would be more familiar and comfortable. Not only had their order of worship and its content not fully come to reflect the new and mixed demographics; but at the same time, the pastor was pursuing ministry in the best way he knew how, in accordance with his training in the African-American tradition. His deep involvement in the life of the community, with several hours spent in meetings in the community, and his social advocacy and activism, were not viewed by the congregation as ministry, because he was seldom in the office! Although this was the largest presenting problem, the worship and other cultural issues mired the pastor-people relationship. First, Riverdale reduced Jackson's remuneration; then a year later, they dismissed him, despite attempts by outside consultants to help both sides understand that the issue was structural, rather than personal. A church, chock-full of potential, with good, energetic, and gifted people, lost an equally good, energetic, and gifted pastor, simply because they thought he was the problem; instead, they might have addressed their issues better had they discovered, understood, and accepted that the church's structure was the fly in the ointment. Jackson himself was not without blame; the ability of leaders to sense structural problems, even if they may not be trained to so articulate them, is a crucial component of wise leadership. Jackson would have served himself and Riverdale well, had he, within his first two or three years of ministry, led the congregation to

11. Ibid., 329.

assess itself, its new realities and the implication of the marvelous diversity the congregation possessed as a rare gift, in the American landscape.

The Riverdale-and-Jackson episode makes the case that there are challenges in the structural mode, which congregations need to surmount successfully. Using nine organizational processes in the structural mode, which Bolman and Deal posit, we are able to appreciate the challenges awaiting congregations who want to be efficient, effective, healthy, and impactful in the structural mode. We cite the first eight here.[12]

1. First, in the process of *strategic planning*, "strategies to set objectives and coordinate resources"[13] are required. This is clearly an administrative challenge. It is not unusual to find board or council meetings, by that or any other name, exhausting their meeting time with concerns about resources: budget, foundation or endowment, buildings, maintenance and the like. Often, though, those same church entities are found wanting in the diligence to spend the requisite time in setting meaningful objectives for the faith community, and managing their resources in a realistic, yet faith-exercising manner, so as to reach those objectives. Obviously, when this is done, the integrity of the church' or denomination's structure is maintained; moreover, the structure is intentional and designed for the entity's realities.

2. Speaking of faith-exercising approaches, the second process is *decision making*, in which a "rational sequence to produce [the] right decision"[14] is required. Faith institutions always face a delicate balance between empirical and scientifically observable facts and faith, which is the "[surety] of what we hope for and [the certainty] of what we do not see."[15] It is important to strike the balance. While one cannot have too much faith, faith never ignores realities; instead, faith acknowledges reality, but seeks to push beyond it, instead of against it. In the final analysis, as was affirmed in the beginning, churches are living organisms, living out the life of Christ, and this is done by faith in Christ. At the same time, they are human organizations, best governed also by rational sequence and logical frameworks.

12. The ninth has to do with economic incentives, an item that may not be applicable to congregational and denominational entities.

13. Bolman and Deal, *Reframing Organizations*, 314.

14. Ibid.

15. Heb 11:1.

3. Thirdly, in the process of *reorganizing*, organizations should "realign roles and responsibilities to fit tasks and environment."[16] Congregations are notorious for scenarios where one person occupies the same position for decades. A man is chair of deacons for thirty years; a woman is treasurer or church clerk or Sunday school secretary for forty. Perhaps this happens because congregational and denominational life are both heavily characterized by volunteer service; and in some cases, volunteers are limited. Perhaps it happens because some congregations lack the imagination for distributing labor in a creative way. Perhaps some congregations lack the courage to remove persons who have long since served out their usefulness or need to make way for others to serve. Whatever the cause, the impact may be more harmful than helpful. Whether it is the entitlement that the long-serving person develops (and the attitudinal deficiencies that accompany it), or the dependency into which others slouch, or the resentment among others who know that someone else can do a better job, the negative results are clear, and the danger to structure is sure. Whatever the fallout, the result is usually a lack of development of the congregation's human capital; and when that is left to fester, the congregation is led into dysfunction.

Apart from cases where the problem is leaving persons to occupy positions way past their termination or rotation date, another common problem to be witnessed in congregations is the square-peg-in-a-round-hole phenomenon, where persons, ranging from somewhat unsuited to thoroughly unsuited for positions, are placed therein anyway. It may happen that, in some cases, when the long-serving person began, he or she was quite suitable; but over the years, the person lost his/her calling, or vision, or energy, or taste for the work, or his/her sense of accountability. He/she may have begun as a round peg in a round hole, but years later, the story became different. Congregations should not wait for the situation to become that dire; instead, regularly scheduled situational and performance evaluation analyses as well as reviews of the development and growth of church members should be undertaken, and the church's ministry goals be reassessed in light of the most current analyses. Congregations and denominations *must* strive for this, no matter how understaffed they might be or how shallow their pool of volunteers.

16. Bolman and Deal, *Reframing Organizations*, 314.

4. Bolman and Deal's fourth process item for organizations in the structural mode is somewhat problematic for congregations, and just hinted at in the last paragraph above: performance *evaluating*. They indicate that it is the "way to distribute rewards or penalties and control performance."[17] This is problematic because, while rewards in the form of recognition and, sometimes, tokens and gifts, do exist in congregational life, penalties—at least for poor functional and organizational performance—are almost unheard of in congregational life. Indeed, there may well be a sense in which, because congregational service is voluntary, penalties for underperformance may be either inappropriate or inapplicable. Of course, penalties and rewards need not be the same measures or instruments in church organizations as might be found in non-church organizations. Nevertheless, it comes down to courage—do congregational and denominational leaders, as they evaluate the progress of ministry and development, have the courage to regulate, encourage, or otherwise control performance, through penalties of any appropriate kind? Do they have the permission of the congregation to do so in the first place? In hierarchical contexts, this might be less problematic than in congregations where greater parity exists between leaders and members, and where, therefore, the environment is egalitarian. It is important, though, where the congregational or denominational culture allows for levying penalties against members, that each leader in those organizations guards against becoming a "petty bureaucrat or tyrant"[18] who, especially in the matter of penalties, becomes vindictive or evil. It is better for such leaders to develop as analysts and architects[19] who help to properly shape the church people's development rather than stifle them. Such leaders should be ones who embrace analysis, and who pursue restructuring where necessary, rather than—in some kind of blissful inaction they might consider to be spiritual—leave everything up to God. Church leaders who opt for the latter, are—no matter how sincere they might be—leading their organizations into dysfunction.

5. The matter of *conflict* and how it is treated is the fifth process. It requires an organization to "maintain organizational goals by having authorities

17. Ibid.
18. Ibid., 356.
19. Ibid.

resolve conflict."[20] Strategies in conflict resolution abound today. And while that was not always so, it does not mean that the church has been bereft of these strategies until they started arising. The Christian faithful should be familiar with Jesus's directive in Matt 18:15–20 for dealing with grievances. The fullest implications of the precept go all the way to verse 35. There, Jesus offers a systematic approach for treating personal grievances (never mind that the interpretation of the final response, when all else fails, is up for grabs, as mentioned in the latter part of verse 17). Communally, there are other examples of conflict management in the New Testament. Acts 6:1–6 as well as 15:1–31 demonstrate the church leaders' skills in heading off conflict. Even the casual reader would appreciate, in each of these three biblical references, the patience, time, and analytical attention to some measure of detail about the issues that attend each scenario. It is a warning to today's Christians living in a sound bite age, not to be impatient of the arduous process involved in pursuing conflict resolution, management, and transformation. Persons familiar with life in congregations might report that they have witnessed a reluctance in some congregations and denominational entities to go through the process of conflict resolution. This, of course, is lamentable, perhaps even a tragedy, since the church ought to be the purveyor of justice and peace.

When Dahlia Crandall became president of the Valencia Fellowship of Churches, she encountered a number of questionable fiduciary issues related to the office of the general secretary. She instructed the fellowship's treasurer to withhold funds to the general secretary who was about to make one of his frequent international trips, and called an emergency meeting of the fellowship's executive committee to investigate the issues. The general secretary, Eric James, was already viewed by many in the churches as haughty and self-serving. But Crandall had found evidence that for several years, James had misappropriated to his own travel *all* the funds meant to be shared among the president and general secretary for travel to international meetings, leaving Crandall and her predecessors at home. When James heard of the financial freeze, he visited Crandall at her home and verbally accosted her there. Because she wanted complete transparency and fairness in the process, after she called the emergency executive committee meeting to order, Crandall vacated the chair and turned the meeting over

20. Ibid., 314.

to Jeff Ramsey, the fellowship's vice president. To her dismay, Ramsey not only cut Crandall off as she attempted to offer her evidence; he also patronized James, thus skewing the platform for fairness. He completely ignored her complaint about James's inappropriate and threatening visit to her home. After a few minutes, James—in one of his usual high-handed displays—got up, declared to the meeting that the fellowship could keep its money since the church over which he was pastor had money. Then he walked out. The matter was never resolved, and Crandall's effectiveness as president waned (while James's bad behavior increased). Justice—not only conflict management—took a hit that day, in the Valencia Fellowship of Churches. When a sense of justice, peace, unity, and reconciliation all break down in a church organization, regardless of whatever else that organization has going for it, it has lost the most crucial part of its structural integrity.

6. The matter of *goal setting*, the sixth process in the structural frame, is about moving the organization in the right direction toward the desired goal.[21] Perhaps this is the most prevalent and common pursuit of congregational and denominational leadership. This is not to say that all such organizations go about it most effectively. We shall visit, in chapter 10, the tenets of good planning that lead an organization in the right direction; but suffice it to say now that congregations would do themselves a world of good as they learn these tenets. These begin with assessing their *values*: that for which they stand and what is really important for them. It continues with clarifying their *vision* of where it is they want to go. It moves to defining their *mission*—that which they are called to do as they seek to reach where they want to go. It matures in mapping out in a strategic plan, outlining how the congregation would move through the paces to complete the mission and reach the goal. These are the main components involved in moving a congregation in the right direction. When congregations master these, their most frequent and likely organizational processes become set to revolutionize their present and future.

7. When organizations *communicate* well, they "transmit facts and information."[22] Doing communication well is one of many challenges that congregations face. In larger congregations, the challenge exists

21. Ibid., 315.
22. Ibid.

for obvious reasons: the greater the size of the congregation, the greater the challenge of communication. Such congregations are able to spend more on various forms of media, but often—just as with smaller churches—there are matters that require the presence of people for the best communication to transpire. In larger churches just as in smaller ones, a congregation is rather lucky to have its entire membership present for special meetings, let alone regular ones, where important decisions are to be made, and where many key pieces of information are generated. Communicating well is the seventh organizational process with which congregations, in the structural mode, should be concerned, and the eighth is closely related.

8. As just noted, congregational meetings are key occasions for creating and conveying facts and information that are germane to the congregation's life. In the structural mode, Bolman and Deal say that, for organizations, *meetings* are "formal occasions for making decisions."[23] Meetings are also the venue for displaying the structure of the organization, as well as determining and designing it, where needed. Parishioners should not forget this, and prove their understanding of how crucial this is by upholding a good attendance record in congregational meetings. Leaders should not forget it either. They should allow full participation from the parishioners, instead of controlling, censuring, and preventing full participation. Their failure to do this allows the congregation to take a structural shape they may not desire, but which, by their actions, they may actually create. The same holds for denominational life: congregations which belong to fellowships, conferences, associations, unions, and/or denominations, should honor their membership by ensuring that they are always well-represented in denominational meetings, so that effective decisions may not only be made, but be celebrated by the entire constituency, as having evolved from the entire constituency.

It should go without emphasis that, in congregations, decision-making should be done with the utmost integrity. Oldbury's approach to appointing new deacons required nominations from the congregation with the deacons making the final choices. Stollmeyer had frequently warned his deacons that, in his church's Baptist polity, the process they were following was improperly reversed. He frequently urged the powerful deacons

23. Ibid.

that they were free to nominate deacons, but that the congregation should elect. But the deacons resisted. Although Stollmeyer repeatedly cited not only denominational polity and convention, but also the scriptural bases for discontinuing the wrong-sided process, it prevailed. One evening when the deacons met to choose new deacons, Stollmeyer observed a few deacons loudly ridiculing and laughingly deriding certain nominees, creating an atmosphere that lacked any grace or Christian charity. Out of shock and sadness, he reminded them that this was to be a prayerful, solemn, serious, and spiritual exercise. This drew, from the chair of the deacons, both a dismissive comment and also a reminder to Stollmeyer that he was a *guest* at the deacons' meeting, and they could, at any time *they* chose, invite him to leave! Many minutes after the voting was ended, the ballots counted, and the new deacons selected, one of the older deacons arrived. Incredibly, the chairman—against Stollmeyer's caution that this was highly irregular and improper—reopened the voting process.

For the sake of structural integrity, congregational meetings of any kind must strive to make decisions with order, propriety, and the best parliamentary practices. Oldbury did not, in this case. It is one of the reasons Oldbury, having lost its structural integrity, became a museum. Healthy structure requires leaders who are committed to rational analysis of their congregations or churches' realities, opportunities, challenges, and resources.

A brief and final word is appropriate with regard to how church leaders become effective analysts. First, they should temper denial with research. By nature, and by virtue of their faith, church people are, generally, optimistic. Sometimes there is a thin line between this optimism and denial. Church people should not deny away tough realities or otherwise avoid discussing them. Some congregations, even when their membership numbers are sharply decreasing, fail to stop, first to grieve the losses, and secondly come to the table to discuss the whys and wherefores, despite being begged to do so. Strong structural leaders (and congregations) temper denial with research. Second, on the other side of the coin, structural leaders should temper hope and faith with reality and resources. Sometimes church people's optimism can become so strong that, while they may escape being in denial about reality, they may fail to adequately harness the resources which, in reality, they *do* have. Third, church people should avoid interchanging denial with hope, or misunderstanding the one for the other. Hope does not deny reality; and reality does not stunt hope. Reality and hope are two sides of the "resource coin" to which people of faith turn, and two cornerstones of the structure they should build.

Chapter 6

Your Church is a Symbolic Entity

CHURCHES ARE PEOPLE; AND wherever people are, symbols are ubiquitous. The very characters you are reading here are symbols of the English language. The writer used icons on his laptop and in the computer applications to produce his manuscript. The dashboard in the vehicle you drove or rode in today contains symbols that guided the driver to reality; as were the road signs and traffic symbols that governed every motorist and pedestrian. The symbols and characters on this page would not be the same if they were written for a Korean readership; so because specific symbols develop within specific cultures, the symbolic frame is also referred to as the cultural frame. This, because the symbols represent the customs, idiosyncrasies, and culture of the communities in which they develop.

Churches and denominational organizations—like people—have personalities and cultures; indeed, their culture and personalities often hold clues for the politics of the entity within which those people commune. Culture—that is, the symbolic frame—is one of the four frames through which a church organization may be viewed, appreciated, and assessed. Perhaps nothing bears out the ambiguity, surprise, and complexity for which Bolman and Deal say organizations are famous, as the symbolic or cultural frame.[1] Hereafter, we may use the two words interchangeably. Considering that that frame goes past what people do and say (and past what the observer sees on the surface) to what the doers and speakers *mean,* one can also assert that the cultural frame alludes to the complexity, deceptiveness, ambiguity and surprise which characterize organizations.[2]

1. See Bolman and Deal, *Reframing Organizations*, 31–32.
2. Ibid.

The symbolic frame is so named because, in organizations, "what is most important is not what happens but what it means."[3] The symbolic frame considers the people who comprise the congregation or denomination, going past their needs, function, teamwork, and communication and the other considerations of the other three frames. It digs *beneath* all of that so as to gain an appreciation of *why* the congregation is what it is, why its people function the way they do and what being who they are means to them. The *why* grows out of meaning that underlies *what* their activities, communications, functions, expressions, celebrations, calendars, and observances all *mean* to them each time they engage (or do not) in any of them. Organizations are often like a kaleidoscope: possible to be defined or even described, but much more fulsomely understood when *experienced*. Organizations—especially church organizations—are understood better through experiencing them and *their* meaning of their experience.

The cultural frame exposes the very powerful notion that organizational meaning may be more important to people than organizational programming. It posits that meaning supersedes what people actually do. It affirms that what matters to them is *how* what they do resonates with their sentiments, values, the familiar, the unarticulated, the felt, the imagined, and the important. The symbolic frame peers into *meaning;* it peers into the symbolism and meaning of what people in organizations say and do. And the symbolic frame understands that "culture forms the superglue that bonds an organization, [and] unites people."[4]

The symbolic frame takes the position that, for those folks within that frame, culture, or in this case, congregation, there is no line drawn between organizational events and their meaning. People create meaning and apply it to events; and therein is the rampant ambiguity that can attend organizations. In order to continue to function in community and in life and to do so meaningfully (or to decide *not* to be involved), people create meaning out of what they do or see being done. Therefore, not only is meaning more important than event, but it is also more important than what they create together, produce together, or even build together. This is culture. Culture can therefore be said to be spiritual; not only from the viewpoint that it goes beyond the tangible to the intangible, and beyond the seen to the unseen, but also because of the comfort, identity, meaning, hope, purpose, and direction for those who share that culture. While other

3. Ibid., 253.
4. Ibid.

lengthy, academic-sounding definitions of culture exist,[5] Bolman and Deal say simply that culture is "the way we do things around here."[6]

In summarizing Bolman and Deal's description of the symbolic frame, it can be said of people in communities or organizations, first, that meaning is more important than meeting, activity, or event; second, people apply meaning to life via symbols and rituals; third, what is *produced from* their activities and events is less important than what is *expressed in* those activities and events; and fourth, their community stories, celebrations, and heroes/heroines ignite passion and more meaning. In all of these, a culture is constructed and that culture, even if undefined, unarticulated, or unmentioned, holds that community or organization together.[7] They refer also to myths[8] which appear to be true stories with a purpose—even if told with embellishments.

INDICATORS OF EFFECTIVENESS IN THE SYMBOLIC FRAME FOR CHURCH ORGANIZATIONS

As a start toward maximizing their effectiveness in the cultural frame, church organizations might consider the following matters. First, the meaning of meetings (general meetings, leadership meetings, committee or board meetings, and yes, even worship meetings): what do church meetings really *mean* beyond what is on the agenda or the order of worship? Second, story-telling: what stories are told in the congregation and by the congregation, and with what purpose and effect? Third, making connections with others—what is the glue that holds the church or the denomination together? Fourth, which congregational events are rituals, containing deeper meaning? Fifth, what does the congregation really mean to its parishioners, or the denomination to its constituent members? And sixth, the organization's culture: what is it, really? What is the organization's "brand" that resonates with its average member? Considering these issues and questions enables discernment and understanding of congregational entities. We focus, briefly, on three of these.

---

5. Consider the many publications of Edgar Schein, a former professor of organizational dynamics at Massachusetts Institute of Technology's Sloan School of Management.

6. Bolman and Deal, *Reframing Organizations*, 269.

7. Ibid., 253.

8. Ibid.

Stories are an indicator of congregational effectiveness and meaningfulness

Church institutions have—if nothing else—a heritage of story-telling. Time and again, the patriarchs and matriarchs of Israel, the forerunner of the Judeo-Christian faith, were told to recount the story of their ancestors' journey to their children.[9] Testimony is part and parcel of this heritage, and at its heart is story-telling. Congregations would do well to include, no matter how high their liturgy, some form of testimony and story-telling in their worship and other meetings. Preaching should reclaim the potency of story; and the church has its own powerful story of Jesus Christ, to be preached. Songs of worship that tell no rich story are unhelpful for developing the faith as well as the community. Congregational and denominational meetings—even the ones of "business" vintage—should be shaped intentionally for telling stories. It is no secret that one prevalent reason for the departure of many from congregations is that church meetings are boring, failing to sufficiently connect attendee with event. Good stories never fail in this way; and stories, if nothing else, bear meaning. "The moral [meaning] of the story" is a phrase that children hear from their earliest storytellers. Meaning should continue to prevail into adulthood; good stories and story-telling accomplish that.

Rituals are an indicator of congregational effectiveness and meaningfulness

Rituals are symbolic acts; each one "invariably alludes to more than it says and has many meanings at once."[10] Organizational scholars suggest that meaning and events are loosely connected. However, on the basis of some church meetings' content and purpose, and how they are run, some church people may be correct in their opinion that those meetings (especially business meetings), are not all the connections needed. Meetings, perhaps *especially* in church organizations, could become rituals, which offer inadequate meaning for participants. "A good deal of . . . corporate planning . . . is like a ritual rain dance; it has no effect on the weather that follows, but those who engage in it think it does. Moreover, it seems to me that much of the advice and instruction related to corporate planning is directed at improving the

9. Exod 12:26; Josh 4:6; 21.

10. Bolman and Deal, *Reframing Organizations*, 261.

dancing, not the weather."[11] Of course, not all church meetings are like that; some churches do succeed in designing meetings that help their members enjoy and value each other and find new ways of doing mission together. Such meetings build connectedness and a sense of family. Susan Gillies,[12] former interim general secretary of the American Baptist Churches USA, remembers a turbulent period in her denomination, prior to her time as general secretary: "We had to affect the weather because the denomination was on the verge of disintegration. I served at a time when there wasn't much time for the dance."[13]

Connectedness is an indicator of congregational effectiveness and meaningfulness

One of the most pervasive indicators and descriptors of congregational effectiveness, as in the symbolic frame, is connectedness. A survey about connectedness and meaning among parishioners and pastors in the American Baptist Churches of Nebraska[14] produced a list that might be true of any congregation or denomination.[15] They listed several items, including the following:

1. Bringing the churches together;
2. The ability to see each other;
3. Enjoying and valuing each other;
4. Doing mission together;
5. Cultivating a sense of family;
6. Forming new relationships;
7. Offering care to another congregation;
8. Facilitating church partnerships;
9. Helping each other in time of need;
10. Encouraging fellowship;

11. Ibid., 302.
12. This is her true name, as well as the institution she led.
13. An interview with Gillies, Summer 2013.
14. This is the institution's true name.
15. These persons were also interviewed during Summer 2013.

11. Affirming and living out *covenant*—not just *membership*; and

12. Encouraging news and stories.

All of these expressions represent the meaning of this church organization to these people.

LEADERSHIP REQUIRED FOR CONGREGATIONS IN THE SYMBOLIC FRAME

Northouse illustrates that, among the roles played by leadership, there are: creating a vision, clarifying the big picture, motivating, inspiring, and energizing and seeking commitment.[16] It may be easily argued that none of these may be accomplished more effectively than by the communication of information that is crafted as story-telling. The latter item—seeking commitment—comes about when people are able to align their doing and giving with meaning and value. Creating vision and clarifying a big picture involves, without doubt, clarifying meaning, which is at the heart of the symbolic frame. Indeed, all of these leader roles either facilitate and/or support the flourishing of values and meaning, both of which are central to keeping people truly connected to a congregation or church organization (itself an aspect of meaning and symbolism), redounding to the organization's strength.

Northouse, as well as other leadership gurus, identify a difference between leadership and management. (We shall explore this difference in chapter 9.) Simply put, management concerns itself with planning and budgeting, organizing and staffing, and controlling[17]—things which maintain the status quo and which often subordinate meaning to function rather than the other way around. Management also tends to subordinate people to purpose, rather than the other way around, or pursuing a healthy synergy between the two. Indeed, this very preference for leadership over management is a symbolic issue: management presides over what *is,* while leadership shoves on toward what *can be.* Admittedly, effective management *does* keep an eye on the future; but because its primary concerns subordinate people to purpose, often with the result of hurting, or discouraging, or dampening the initiative of people, it does not go the distance into the future, toward what *can be,* as leadership can. It is true that meaning resides in what is, but it can become fossilized there; however, in what

16. Northouse, *Leadership Theory*, 12.

17. Ibid.

can be, meaning can take wings! Any organization—especially a service organization, and more so, a spiritual organization—should prefer wings over fossils. We have all seen management at work in church life: the boring and lengthy meetings discussing finance, fundraising, membership decline, building maintenance, minutes from the last meeting, correction of minutes, discussing the next bake-sale, or garage sale, and so on. Leadership, though, is consumed with the future, with what could be, and with new, adaptive, and strategic thinking, and new pursuits, regardless of how demanding. Although congregations and denominations require management at some points, they should be outfitted, predominantly, primarily, and robustly, with leadership much more than management.

Transformational leadership

The symbolic frame requires for church organizations, first and foremost, transformational leaders. Northouse's affirmation that transformational leadership gets out of people "more than what is usually expected of them"[18] may leave one asking, "Whose expectations?" and "By whose or what measure?" Avolio and Bass are equally imprecise when they say that "*Transformational* leaders motivate others to do more than they originally intended and often even more than they thought possible."[19] They too, leave the reader to wonder whether the pronoun "they" refers to the leaders or the others. Either could be true. Transformational pastors or church leaders pursue mutually cooperative relationships with others; even in a hierarchical setting, such leaders would view their subordinates more as partners than subordinates. In such a context, meaning and symbolism already prevail; because *how* leaders consider and conduct themselves becomes symbolic and definitive of the nature of the leadership they offer, creating meaning in the subordinates of the organization itself. When a leader works with others as partners—rather than as subjects, or as targets, or as managed subordinates, or worse, as adversaries—such leadership has the propensity to be transformational, bearing a special meaning to all partners, conducive to team-building and community building. In that case the transformational leader actually symbolizes this team spirit and sense of community!

If one were to improve on Northouse and Avolio and Bass (in saying more about what is usually or originally expected), one might define

18. Ibid., 185.

19. Avolio and Bass, *Developing Potiential*, 1.

transformational leadership as that which ignites people to move beyond previous limits; and when they have done that, to motivate them to do it again, going even further the next time. This definition squares with what has been observed earlier: that if leadership (instead of management) gives congregations and church organizations wings rather than fossils, then *transformational* leadership, all the more, keeps churches constantly pursuing, seeking, and understanding meaning. It keeps churches aligning *doing* and *saying* with *meaning*. This occurs in the organization, singularly as a unit, and severally among its members and participants. Meaning involves feeling—the deep emotions and values felt within a person. Transformational leadership "is concerned with emotions, values, ethics, standards and long-term goals[20]"—some of the same phenomena with which the symbolic frame concerns itself. This strengthens the case for transformational leadership as the most suitable and appropriate leadership choice for the symbolic frame.

Transformational leadership involves, among other things, phenomena such as charisma, and what leadership experts refer to as the four I's: idealized influence, inspirational motivation, intellectual stimulation, and individualized consideration.[21] These we shall visit in detail in chapter 8. Briefly, though, *idealized influence* is otherwise called charisma because it involves the leader's displayed and genuine interest in the follower-partners. This interest is communicated through genuine (authentic) care, listening, and empathy. This should be easy for church leaders, if only because they seek to imitate Jesus; however, this quality needs to be understood also as a principle of leadership theory. Care, listening and empathy all form the fertile ground for uplifting stories to be told—stories that bolster the congregation's culture—for meaning to be engendered, and values reinforced. The follower-partners, in turn, develop trust in and respect for the leaders, and cooperate with them. The transformational leaders, in turn, use this capital to spread the superglue of common vision, values, and purpose throughout the church, building unity and strength around that meaning. Transformational leaders "talk about . . . values, beliefs, purposes, a collective mission, and the benefits of trusting each other."[22] In the symbolic frame, story-telling may be the best vehicle for these talks.

20. Northouse, *Leadership*, 185.

21. See Northouse, *Leadership*; Gill, *Theory*; and Sosik and Jung, *Full-range Leadership*.

22. Sosik and Jung, *Full Range Leadership*, 15.

This segues into *inspirational motivation,* which needs no elaboration of its self-evident meaning. Congregational and denominational stories, embellishments, fairy tales, myths, ceremonies, and rituals should all inspire motivation within the organization. Third, *intellectual stimulation* also finds its home in the symbolic frame. Transformational leaders "question the *status quo.*"[23] Finding meaning and deciphering symbols and rituals is as much an intellectual exercise as it is an emotional one. It requires intellectual stimulation to cut through the ambiguity that attends the multitude of meanings that reside in the multitude of people in church organizations. "The symbolic frame interprets and illuminates the basic issues of meaning and belief that make symbols so powerful . . . facing uncertainty and ambiguity, people create symbols to resolve confusion, find direction, and anchor hope and faith."[24] These acts of interpretation, illumination and resolution all require intellectual stimulation. Faith in Christ may be motivation; but while it is not being suggested that faith by itself is inadequate, congregational leaders and parishioners would do well to understand that since faith without works is dead,[25] intellectual stimulation motivates people toward works. Indeed, all of these—idealized influence, inspirational motivation, and intellectual stimulation—are best exercised as the transformational leader engages in the fourth I: *individualized consideration.* Gill describes this as "management by wandering around."[26] Although Gill, perhaps unfortunately, uses the word *management* to address a *leadership* function, it is clear that this "wandering around" is meant to involve giving and receiving feedback, sharing and listening to stories, and building common culture and meaning through all the organization's strata of people, with a view to giving deep consideration to individuals—real people—more than programs, deadlines, and the bottom line.

According to Northouse, three of the five effective leader practices that Kouzes and Posner summarize merit attention as practices required for effective leadership in the symbolic frame: *inspire a shared vision, challenge the process,* and *encourage the heart.*[27] In these three initiatives, effective leadership comes alive in the symbolic frame. They all relate to the mind and heart, meaning and culture, and emphasize the link—though loose—between doing

23. Gill, *Theory,* 84.

24. Bolman and Deal, *Reframing Organizations,* 253.

25. Jas 2:17.

26. Gill, *Theory,* 84.

27. See Northouse, *Leadership,* 198–99.

and meaning. They are uncannily spiritual, prophetic, pastoral, and commu-nal, as though tailor-made for church organizations! And if communal and pastoral (as in a shepherd leading sheep aright) they are indeed, tantamount to "leading people into the future."[28] Transformational leadership certainly presents as a hand-and-glove leadership choice for the symbolic frame, and especially in congregational and denominational life.

Servant leadership

Servant leadership certainly stands as an eligible contender for effective congregational leadership, even if only because servant leadership gives the leader power to *model* the organization's values, purpose, culture, and overall meaning to the member-followers. Because servant leaders are ac-tive participants among the parishioners or denominational constituents, they may even create new symbols and rituals to intellectually stimulate the faithful on a path to develop or reinterpret meaning. Here, one of Greenleaf's ten characteristics of servant leadership is crucial: conceptual-ization.[29] By virtue of this characteristic, servant leaders are visionary; but if they are also transformational leaders (of whom an important skill and role is empowering others) they may also enable or empower their followers to conceptualize, dream, shape, and reshape meaning. The ability to do this in church life, and the dazzling potential they afford, cannot be overstated.

INDICATORS OF LEADER EFFECTIVENESS IN THE SYMBOLIC FRAME

Given the types of leadership required for the symbolic frame, our attention turns now to the realities, markers, and behaviors that are demonstrative of effective leadership in this frame.

1. Symbolic leaders have a keen sensitivity to and for symbols and sym-bolism. They are interested in the meaning that followers find in the organization, and the symbols, rituals, and stories they use to express or reinforce that meaning. They investigate these symbols and mean-ings, interpreting them so as to enhance their leadership effectiveness. They encourage and facilitate followers to coalesce, rally, and unify

28. Bolman and Deal, *Reframing Organizations*, 260.

29. See Northouse, *Leadership*, 222.

around their varieties of meanings, while seeking to find the single thread or glue that holds the organization together *via* the multitude of meanings. The Christian faith and church are both replete with symbols, ranging from the cross, to baptism, to candles. Even the format of sanctuary seating and the arrangement of the platform, podium, pulpit, altar, or whatever that area at the front of the sanctuary is called in whichever tradition, is full of symbolism and meaning. These things do not necessarily mean the same thing to each parishioner; yet, they all coalesce around those various meanings! There is a treasure trove of possibilities for the congregation, whose congregational leader seeks to explore these meanings with the congregation.

2. Symbolic leaders tell stories and credible myths that declare the value of the organization. They create opportunities for followers to tell *their* stories, which express meaning, renew inspiration, uncover their valued symbols and rituals, and contribute to deepening commitment to the organization on the part of followers and leaders, alike. Sermons, whatever their genre or content, should tell *a* story, even if not *stories*. Hymns and songs should weave a progressive story of some kind; and worship designers might do well to avoid truncating hymns, an act which often distorts the story told therein; they should also watch out for songs that *ad nauseam* (to some) repeat some nice-sounding phrase with no story, or an interrupted story. The whole worship experience—whether liturgically high or low—should weave a communal story. It is these stories which, over time, build the congregation's culture and its unique identity.

3. Symbolic leaders, in the context of church organizations, build faith and hope among the faithful, and point them to the future. They communicate to them that their organization is valuable and serves a crucial purpose in their lives and world. They influence their followers, parishioners, members and member congregations toward organizational commitment by communicating the undergirding ideals of the organization; they motivationally inspire them; and they intellectually stimulate them through personal and individual interaction, as far as possible. They inspire a common and hopeful vision of the organization's future, and urge followers toward *more* "than . . . is usually expected of them."[30]

30. Ibid., 185.

4. Symbolic leaders embody and model the organization's values. They live the organization's purpose and tell the organization's story through their own lives and conduct. They sufficiently differentiate between themselves and their organization so as to avoid thinking that they *are* the organization; yet, they understand that they must embrace and model the organization's values. This is a lesson that Terry Fellowes, pastor of Ocean View (the "kingdom" that we saw in chapter 1) evidently failed to learn. It is a lesson that appears to be discarded in too many contemporary congregations and church organizations, where critics with a keen eye may be able to notice key leaders who appear unable to differentiate between themselves and the organization. This may be a megachurch on the one hand, or a smaller congregation on the other. Images of Jim Jones's People's Temple, or David Koresh's Branch Davidians, come quickly to mind.

5. Symbolic leaders come alongside their followers; it is a fitting spiritual description of leadership, since this is what the *Paraclete*, the Holy Spirit,[31] does. They consider themselves the "first among models" rather than the first among equals, or worse: high, among all others who are lesser! They function as lateral partners rather than hierarchical bosses; they operate among, rather than above, the organization's people, followers, and stakeholders. Indeed, any spiritual, congregational, or denominational leaders who are not characterized by any of this open themselves to the charge of being either bogus or inappropriate for church organizations. As well, they may be set to become— or already are—toxic leaders whom the church cannot afford, if such leaders are to be models of the Christ himself. In that regard, "bogus", "fraudulent" or even "dangerous" are not inappropriate or hyperbolic descriptors. Unfortunately, these are not unheard of in (too many) church and denominational contexts.

6. Symbolic church leaders lead their organizations to guard against emotionalism without reality, ceremony without sincerity, and spirituality without action. They know that meaning, no end in itself, is tethered to what is *done* even if the meaning is, according to this theory, more important to the organization's members than what is done. This only demands a greater detail to the truths and reality which undergird the meaning; and such leaders would pay perhaps even more attention to

31. See John 14:16, 26.

the former than the latter, so as to ensure that the latter emanates from responsible and solid foundations.

7. Symbolic leaders advocate for the organization's viability, especially among marginal followers. They explore, with marginal members, what aspects of the organization's meaning for them—or lack of meaning thereof—has or has not contributed to their being on the periphery. They promote and advocate for the organization's vision, purpose, and life, and promote the superglue of meaning that holds the organization together. They investigate the factors that neutralize that glue among marginalized followers with a view to renewing or fostering engagement; and they enable the organization's members to tell the story and to tell its meaning; and then to live out, embody, and demonstrate both story and meaning to new recruits. These are crucial for congregations and church organizations which depend on a lively and life-giving membership, and on the addition of new partners in ministry and mission, who would share the organization's meaning and culture.

PART II

Leadership that Transforms Congregations

He who was seated on the throne said, "I am making everything new!"
—*Rev 21:5, NIV*

See, I am doing a new thing! Now it springs up; do you not perceive it?
—*Isa 43:19, NIV*

Things do not change; we change.
—*Henry David Thoreau, "Walden"*

Chapter 7

New Wine for New Wineskins

CHURCH PEOPLE, CHURCH INSTITUTIONS, and their organizations, which do not desire to be led into dysfunction, should take a long look at the decades of leadership theory, and decide for themselves what new lessons lie in those old theories, and even seek to imagine new theories or lessons of their own. It was the founder of the church (Jesus) who declared that one does not place new wine into old wineskins,[1] unless one wants a mess, with all the immature wine spilled and wasted. Leadership theory has been around for over one hundred years. Scholars have traced leadership definitions, and explored many of those theories from 1900 through to the 1980s.[2] On that century-old basis, leadership studies can be described as old; however, compared to other disciplines such as medicine or astrology, leadership studies as a discipline is relatively new. Even though many of the theories defined in the past hundred years are now passé, there remains in leadership studies new "wine" for congregations and church organizations seeking better ways. Leadership studies offer much for church organizations seeking renewal, robust ministry, and stronger leadership and structuring, into the twenty-first century.

There is a broad swath of leadership theories with a variety of names which may mean nothing to the uninitiated: traits theory; skills theory; style, psychodynamic, situational, contingency, path-goal, leader-member exchange, servant, authentic, and transformational theories. All of these demonstrate the breadth of the study of leadership theory; and these are not all the theories that may exist! Neither are some of these theories particularly useful for congregational contexts as others may be. Leadership

1. Matt 9:17.
2. See Rost, *Leadership*, 37–95.

theories are not only numerous; they are also divisible among many different paradigms: *positivist* (or *functionalist*, which considers leaders' function without considering ethics); *social constructivism* (which considers
the context in which leaders function, but is unconcerned with how they
use power); *critical* (which examines leadership from the perspective of
authority and control); and *postmodern* (which goes past the modern era's
ideas of fixity, tradition, order, and what is expected).[3] The *postmodern*
theory of leadership pursues ideas of contingency (flexibility), ambiguity,
complexity, and the unpredictability of human behavior and relationships,
and the way they all come to have impact in leadership scenarios. Each of
the theories above, in its own era, was or is certainly paradigmatic, and
each has contributed meaningfully to the development and state of leadership. Each brings fascinating perspectives, and together they form a strong
tapestry for understanding leadership. More than that, these paradigms
together have formed an even stronger platform from which any further
study of leadership may be launched, because each leaves questions that remain unanswered, even though each may be said to have arisen in response
to the questions the previous one left unanswered. Such is the nature of
leadership study—it is a moving target, as dynamic as the church itself,
ever-changing, because of the dynamic Holy Spirit and the pursuit of truth
and excellence by the people who comprise the church.

Each paradigm pushes the envelope further, questions assumptions
more aggressively, and considers the issues more broadly. So, for example,
the traits theory assumed that it was either a great man who made history
or it was history that made a man great (despite the fact that back then, evidence abounded that women could be great too), and that this is what made a
leader great. The postmodern paradigm of leadership, however, goes beyond
these assumptions, beyond a single individual, and beyond a single locale.
Yes, leadership studies and leadership theory have come a long way, and the
church has much to gain from learning leadership theory.

So, what *can* the church learn from leadership studies? It is known
that leadership definitions abound, but none is adequate, by itself, to define
leadership; leadership scholars always take care to note how elusive leadership definitions are. Leadership theories are equally elusive; this is why they
are called theories, in the first place. They are quite tentative, though that
assertion should not be misconstrued to suggest that they are useless, or
deficient, or to be held with disregard or suspicion. Leadership theories and

3. Kezar et al., "Rethinking," 15–29.

definitions abound, and even when they are taken together, they are inadequate for completely defining leadership. Scholars know this very well. "No theory or model of leadership . . . has provided a full and satisfactory explanation of leadership."[4]

All that said, leadership scholars are relentless, careful, and astute, and are always aiming at clarity, if not accuracy. Leadership assumptions are constantly being questioned, and no theory is taken for granted any longer. Northouse treats every leadership theory with an examination of their strengths and criticisms, adequacies and inadequacies, as well as their applications.[5] He cites each theory's limitations, warning leadership scholars and practitioners alike about the fluidity of leadership theories, definitions, and parameters; but at the same time, he encourages them to take the paradigms further and even create new paradigm shifts. Gill treats leadership theories with the same approach of questioning, with a critique of each theory.[6] Even the supposed flagship of leadership theory—transformational leadership—is questioned by Bass and Steidlmeier, who find that ethical criticisms can be made, even of transformational leadership![7] Postmodernists question it too.[8] So nothing can be taken for granted, and the leadership student must remain alert. Leadership study is in flux, still developing, and is therefore fluid; and because of it, leadership study is interesting and exciting.

What all of this suggests is that the church is free to develop thoughtful models of leadership, which either resemble, draw from, or are extensions of models, theories, and definitions which already exist, or completely new ones, if possible—notwithstanding that the church's scriptures warn that there is nothing new under the sun.[9] This is an exciting proposition. But before jumping to models, perhaps congregations might conduct deep reflection on their realities in order to develop theories and definitions of leadership. This reflection might help them understand the dynamics of their congregations. As well, any theories and definitions of leadership they devise would flow from their thoughtful observation of their congregations.

---

4. Gill, *Theory*, 63.

5. See Northouse, *Leadership*. Each chapter, from 2 through 16, takes that approach.

6. See Gill, *Theory*, 62–107.

7. Bass and Steidlmeier, "Ethics," 192.

8. Kezar et al., "Rethinking," 24.

9. Eccl 1:9.

THE SHEPHERD-FLOCK THEORY OF LEADERSHIP

Consider, for example, what we may call the *shepherd-flock* theory of leadership.[10] This theory asserts that parishioners are motivated, less by their community's vision, purpose, values, and ideals, and more by their own individual wants, needs, opinions, imaginations, and delights. This is not an attempt at pessimism; this is the result of carefully considered praxis in a vast and lengthy experience in congregational life, and a theology of leadership arising therefrom.

The images of sheep in scriptures—one of the primary metaphors for the faithful in Christ, the Shepherd—demonstrate that sheep roam and become lost,[11] likely because they are primarily guided by their hunger, thirst, and needs, which cause them to stray in search of satisfying these needs, even if it means separating from the rest of the flock, both deliberately and inadvertently. In this *shepherd-flock* theory of leadership, parishioner-followers are guided by a lower hierarchy of values and needs, in which their own needs supersede the community's. Kellerman observes that "leaders lead and followers follow not out of the kindness of their collective hearts but because it is in their self-interest."[12] In this *shepherd-flock* theory, the leader leads, not so much a homogeneous community, as much as she or he leads a group of disparate, but organizationally related, individuals whose greater commitment is to their individual goals than to the community's broader goals. In this context, the leader is successful and effective, more on the basis of meeting individual, intermediate, and lower goals which answer individuals' fancies, and less on the basis of pursuing larger, ultimate goals that serve the community; this, especially if those goals require the followers' surrender of individual goals.

Wherever *shepherd-flock* realities (according to this theory) are at work, transformational leadership may be necessary. Bass and Steidlmeier refer to scholars who "see transformational leaders as subversive, because transformational leaders encourage members of an organization to go beyond their own self-interests for the good of the organization. As a consequence, the members lose more than they gain."[13] Those scholars assume that such members "sacrifice their own interests in order to conform to the

---

10. This is this author's own original leadership theory.
11. Matt 18:12–13; Luke 15:4.
12. Kellerman, "How Bad Leadership Happens," 42.
13. Bass and Steidlmeier, "Ethics," 204.

leaders' vision of what will be best for the organization."[14] But when vision is properly discerned, formulated, and articulated, it is never only the leaders' vision; instead, it is an organic and communal vision, born from deeply engaging the members in the process. Unfortunately, when in some congregations, transformational leaders emphasize community values as priority over wayward and self-serving individual needs, some people disengage and leave the congregation, deeming, not so much that the congregation's values are inconvenient, but that their American, or western, or adult freedom is impinged upon. The same thing happens at the denominational level, where congregations, unwilling to work with the denomination's wider community objectives, disconnect from the denomination when they feel that their autonomy, or freedom, or organizational choices, are at stake.

Johnsonville Faith Community is a congregation in mid-America where, it is said, passive aggressiveness and individualism thrive at higher levels than normal. When Carter Murray took over the reins of Johnsonville, he and the lay leaders pursued a strong theme of community; after all, the church bore this very word in their name! Murray had sensed the members' individualism, manifested in their strong inclination to "do their own thing". Within twelve months, Johnsonville lost 30 percent of its membership. In a leaders' meeting, called to analyze this phenomenon, it was affirmed by all that, chief among the many culprits, was congregational resistance to the challenge to join community rather than pursue one's own business. Indeed, according to their leadership consulting agency, Johnsonville's organizational archetype was *everyperson,* one trait of which is that their members could become highly individualistic, in pursuit of their own plans.

Leadership theory suggests that, in order for Murray to have prevented more persons from leaving, he could have, despite being a transformational leader, performed leadership in the *contingency* (or *situational*) mode, meaning, as the name suggests, "there is no one best style of leadership . . . leaders will use different styles according to the nature of the situation and the followers."[15] However, Murray would have had to do this constantly in contingency mode, to the extent that he could no longer be defined as a transformational leader. Because of his constant adjustment to what others wanted, rather than pursuing the steady ideals of the congregation, Murray's own authenticity as a leader might have been challenged (as well, perhaps, as his sanity), in addition to having to face the temptation to

14. Ibid.
15. Gill, *Theory*, 62.

be *pseudotransformational,* by virtue of giving wayward and self-focused people what they wanted, and what was popular, rather than what was right and good for all, and for the beloved community. Church leaders should always guard against this kind of approach so as to secure cheap coopera- tion, growth, and claims to success; for there is no healthy transformation in pseudo leadership. The *shepherd-flock* idea is merely a theory of con- gregational and denominational leadership, discovered, unfortunately, in many congregations and denominations. It is certainly not recommended as a model of leadership. There are better ways!

THEORIES OF LEADERSHIP AND THE CHURCH

What can the church learn from leadership studies? Current, contempo- rary, and postmodern approaches to leadership studies and leadership the- ory involve *people* and relationships. Leadership study is now completely entrenched in the study of human relationships and human responsibility, and that is just where it is supposed to be. Long before it is about programs and systems, techniques and strategies, it is about relationships—just as is the church. But leadership theory studies are concerned not only with what relationships *are* but also with what the *perceptions* of relationships and leadership dynamics are, and in what contexts. There is assigned leader- ship—leaders who are *appointed*—as well as emergent leadership—those who are *anointed*—who, like King David, Jesse's last son, emerged not only above his brothers, but emerged through his experiences of killing a lion and leading flocks of sheep.[16] There is personal leadership and rela- tional leadership. Leadership study produces a certain perspective when investigated from the viewpoint of an individual, and quite another when viewed from the angle of the community. Leadership can be understood as shared; and it can be understood as hierarchical, where some kind of predetermined, or preset, or conventional, or imagined, or artificial lines of partition exist within a group of people that define one or more as leaders, and the others as followers. Where these lines exist, the leaders might *say* that their followers are equal to them; yet there remains, in reality, some notion or evidence of inequality—but with connectivity—between the two. Leadership studies include the examination of the dynamics of the inequal- ity within such groups, sometimes with a view to removing the inequality, or sometimes to understand why that inequality may in fact be already

16. 1 Sam 16–17.

absent. All of these considerations present a treasure-trove of foundations for church organizations to consider and from which to craft healthy leadership exchange between leaders and those who cooperate with leaders.

Churches and denominational organizations would want to think twice about leadership that is interpreted as one individual using or seeking to coerce or induce others to do what he or she wants. On the other hand, church organizations which subscribe to the New Testament command to "submit to one another out of reverence for Christ"[17] would choose to pursue leadership which is about relationships *between all* the persons in an organization. Even then, church leaders would need to determine to what extent leadership theories, which address relationships that are based on reward, apply in church; or to what extent they are based on mutual correction both in good and bad times, or on intervention only when problems arise. Church leaders should consider the value of leadership based on earned respect, partnership, and mutuality. They should examine the difference between the potential results of leadership based on one person's vision, versus those that may arise from many people's collective vision.

Church organizations and denominations may be inspired to new and reframed thinking about leadership, given Rost's patient research which reveals that *leader* and *leadership* are not interchangeable terms,[18] and that *leadership* does not reside in, or define, one person. Instead, leadership refers to process and relationships, and the dynamics between people who intend to pursue common goals together, especially the goals of a greater leader, Jesus Christ, Lord of the church. Church leaders know that those goals may be determined and reached in a variety of ways and for a variety of motives and purposes.

The prevalence and danger of the great man theory of leadership in churches

Many Christians' introduction to the faith and to the church would have been through Sunday school. There, as the stories of the Bible were told, many would have had their first introduction—whether wittingly or unwittingly—to the *great man* theory of leadership. This theory, also known as the theory of the heroic leader, is central to what is also referred to as the traits theory. The *great man* theory considers "the innate qualities and

17. Eph 5:21.
18. Rost, *Leadership*, 41–43.

characteristics possessed by great social, political, and military leaders (e.g., Catherine the Great, Mohandas Gandhi, Indira Gandhi, George Washington, Joan of Arc, and Napoleon Bonaparte). It was believed that people were born with these traits, and that only *great* people possessed them."[19] Having been developed in the early twentieth century, by the middle of that century, the theory was practically debunked. "Rather than being a quality that individuals possess, leadership was reconceptualized as a relationship between people in a social situation."[20]

Still, perhaps because of Sunday school, or because of the prevalence of greatness in the many stories and episodes in the Bible, or perhaps because of how these stories and situations have been interpreted and communicated, it is undeniable that *great man* ideas still prevail in church circles, even into the twenty-first century. Indeed, it can even be asserted that *great man* ideas have been infamously rampant in church, whether one refers to popes with papal authority (and sometimes political and imperial authority!) or to megachurch and so-called televangelical personalities in America's recent past and present. Whether the great men range from Billy Graham to Sun Myung Moon, or from Pat Robertson to Jim Jones, or from Oral Roberts to Jerry Falwell, or from T. D. Jakes to Terry Fellowes in chapter 1, the *great man* theory is very much alive in the American church. And so-called "great" women are not to be left out, be it Jan Crouch, or Tammy Faye Baker, or Joyce Meyer, or Mother Angelica, or Paula White, or Ellen G. White, or Juanita Bynum.

Indeed, it invites investigation as to whether it is the *great man* theory, more than any so-called evangelical moorings, which caused many American evangelicals to get on the bandwagon of the person who became the forty-fifth president of the United States, despite his lack of the knowledge, credentials, decorum, and decency usually required of presidential candidates, and despite his propensity to disruption and scandal. This individual's colorfulness, uniqueness, so-called political incorrectness (or irreverence and obscenity, some might say), and braggadocio, plus his very slogan—to make America *great* again—remain attractive to any, for whom the *great man* theory remains valid. All of this supersedes their concern about any dangers that attend his tenure, dismissing the leadership rethinking that has debunked the same *great man* theory. Admittedly, if all of this is indeed so, it might be said that these people are not following a theory; instead, they are

19. Northouse, *Leadership*, 19.
20. Ibid.

perpetuating a phenomenon, in which there is danger. This danger is—despite any interpretations of the Old or even New Testament—more prevalent in church circles. Anything that smacks of the *great man* theory, or the practice of it in church, is to be deemed counterproductive to the church as a body, and to the sound development of its leadership. It should be viewed, also, as a recipe for congregational and denominational dysfunction.

POWER

One of the most palpable aspects of leadership, especially so in church circles, is power. Religion and faith issues revolve around power. Many people of the Christian faith begin their prayers with the two words "Almighty God." Many effective leaders or speakers within the faith are referred to as *dynamic*, a derivative of the Greek word, *dunamis*, meaning power. If nothing else, leadership is about power. Bad leadership, toxic leadership, despotism, autocracy, dictatorship, or any other such form of harmful leadership are all due to the misuse or abuse of power. "Power is the capacity or potential to influence. People have power when they have the ability to affect others' beliefs, attitudes, and courses of action."[21] Power resides in, and is used by, people. This is one reason that leadership theory identifies two sources of power as *position power* and *personal power.*

Position and personal power

Position power, as the name implies, relates to the leveraging of influence over others on the basis of one's authority position, as perceived by both the leader and the followers—authority that reposes in the leader's organizational position. So a pastor might, on the sheer basis of her position as pastor, be the embodiment of power to parishioners who perceive her as a figure of authority. Personal power, though similarly residing in the leader, is not, however, related to the leader's position; instead it relates to the leader's own personal qualities, abilities, and equipment for the position she or he holds.

21. Ibid., 9.

Legitimate and coercive power in church circles

Among the various types of position power that Gill notes are two that warrant mention here: legitimate and coercive power.[22] Legitimate power flows from the leader's authority, as perceived by the follower, which influences the follower to comply with the leader's vision, guidance, requests, or directive. Usually this is power reposing in the leader which motivates the follower, by the follower's own volition, to respond to the leader's authority. When this influence becomes forceful, and where the leader deliberately uses this authority to make the follower do something, this power becomes coercive. Gill observes of coercive power that it is "the perceived ability of a leader or manager to bring about undesirable or unpleasant outcomes for those who do not comply with expectations, instructions, or directives."[23]

We raise these two aspects of position power because each represents a different side of the coin of leadership in congregational and denominational institutions. One of them looks more like the leadership Jesus exercised with his disciples, and the other does not. Even where Jesus was seen instructing his disciples to do something, it was always in the context of Jesus's legitimate power—a power that always seemed to invite, propel, and eventually compel the disciple to comply with Jesus's commands because they were already enamored with and mesmerized by his (legitimate) power and authority, and subscribed to the values inherent in his legitimacy. Indeed, the disciples marveled at Jesus's authority while embracing it,[24] while others marveled at it while questioning it![25] On the basis of the foregoing, it would be fair to say that any pastoral or episcopal or denominational authority that relies often or purely on coercive power to motivate parishioners can reasonably be interpreted to be improper, inappropriate, perhaps even suspect, and certainly unreflective of the Christ, whom such authorities claim to imitate or represent. Many church leaders appear to gravitate to the use of coercive power. Many do so on the basis of claimed spiritual superiority and an ability to hear God better than anybody else, or even exclusively to anyone else. Some others do so because they are considered the one person from whom the church's vision for the future should emanate. Whatever the motivation or basis, we allow Northouse the

22. Gill, *Theory*, 266–67.
23. Ibid., 267.
24. See Matt 8:27.
25. See Matt 21:23.

final warning on the inappropriateness of, and dangers attending, coercive power: "Leaders who use coercion are interested in their own goals and seldom are interested in the wants and needs of subordinates. Using coercion runs counter to working *with* followers to achieve a common goal."[26]

Three aspects of personal power: referent, expert and information power

We turn, for moments, to the matter of personal power, three germane aspects of which are *referent*, *expert* and *information* power.[27] *Referent* power can be said to be influence, leveraged upon followers by a leader, in accordance with the leader's likeability, sensitivity for the followers' concerns, and from the esteem with which the followers hold the leader. If the followers believe that the leader really cares for them, their needs, and their development, and if that belief is ignited by the leader's demonstrated care for the followers, then this could be described as referent power.

Expert power, as the name implies, refers to the leader's expertise, competence, and professionalism, with regard to his or her calling, work requirements, and performance, as perceived by followers. For pastors and congregational operatives, this might include their expertise at pastoring, counseling, preaching, administrating, managing, encouraging, leading, coaching, correcting, equipping, inspiring, and more.

Information power, again as the name implies, has to do with the leader's power, as perceived by followers, arising from the leader's knowledge about his or her work. Additionally it is a little more than that: it extends to information that followers or supporters need, but do not have, but which the leader has.[28] Clearly, in congregational, denominational and faith institutions, this is of paramount importance. Pastors, congregational, and denominational leaders are expected to address matters of faith and practice, interpret the faith, and lead others to interpret the faith. This is why they are expected to either attend seminary or otherwise immerse themselves in biblical and theological development and formation, or be demonstrably gifted in these areas of knowledge. This is why, even if they benefitted from formal theological education, it is highly recommended that they continue in an ongoing— even if informal—college of learners. This might be continuing education

26. Northouse, *Leadership*, 11 (emphasis his).

27. Gill, *Theory*, 268-69

28. Ibid., 269.

in the form of courses of postgraduate study, or some informal and regular gathering of ministry colleagues or leaders for the continuing development of their proficiency and intelligence for church leadership.

Empowerment

An old pop song says that what the world needs now is love, sweet love. A little Sunday school song echoes back that it's love that makes the world go 'round. While there might be no disagreement, it might be also affirmed that among the primary things that make other things go, make people move, and therefore what people need, is power. In a biblical, theological, and ecclesiological sense, love is easily understood as power. Simply put, "effective leaders empower people to be able to do what needs to be done."[29] A car's motor is the source of its power. But without a transmission to transfer power from the motor to the wheels, that car goes nowhere. A leader's power is like a car's motor. Empowerment is like the transmission, through which the leader transfers and shares power with his partner-followers, enabling the whole organization to move and work; and of course, at the speed determined by the transmission!

Empowerment is neither delegation of responsibilities nor division of labor; so we should be careful to make that distinction. Empowerment goes further than simply apportioning responsibilities to others. Going further to allow autonomy for decision-making might seem like empowerment, but it is not yet empowerment. Blanchard adds that true empowerment requires, beyond autonomy, "replacing hierarchy with self-managing teams."[30] Empowerment explores every possible meaning of sharing power, to the extent that it alerts the leader that leadership does not reside only in her or him, but that it also resides in how every single member of the organization shares in locating, distributing, redistributing, allocating, and exercising that power. It involves determining the gifts, talents, and abilities of every member in the organization and committing to create avenues for these gifts and talents to be utilized to the benefit of the whole organization and to the fulfillment of the organization's mission. It involves a commitment to engage every member, both in determining the shape of that mission in the first place, and in the requisite and prior process of clarifying the organization's values and imagining its vision.

29. Ibid., 231.
30. Ibid., 237.

Empowerment aims, as far as possible, to involve every member of an organization in sharing the power involved in gathering information, learning, experimenting, questioning, critiquing, visioning, reframing, planning, developing, and executing the organization's mission. It involves sharing both the credit and joys that come the organization's way in times of success, as well as their pain and resolve when success has been delayed, rather than placing blame on one or two scapegoats. The Christian value, "when one member suffers, all suffer; and when one rejoices, all rejoice,"[31] can be easily seen from all of this. The principle of empowerment appears tailor-made for congregational and denominational life, vitality, effervescence, and effectiveness.

The episode in Exod 18 presents an interesting case study. Moses is overburdened with the task of hearing the people's cases and judging them from morning till evening, day after day. He has a fortuitous visit from his father-in-law Jethro, who observes the situation and challenges Moses about what he, Jethro, obviously thinks is madness! "What you are doing is not good . . . you will only wear yourself out. The work is too heavy for you; you cannot handle it alone."[32] Jethro recommends that Moses find capable men from among the entire constituency, among whom he should share the responsibilities. Moses listens, and appoints what appears to be several hundreds of judges to share the work. It is for the reader to determine whether this is a case of empowerment or delegation; if the former, does it reflect the ramifications discussed above? And if the latter, what could have been done to make the process true empowerment and not merely delegation?

Or consider the negotiations between Nelson Mandela and Frederik de Klerk ahead of the former's release from prison in 1989. Even before de Klerk took office, Pieter Botha and his regime were attempting to negotiate with Mandela, while he was still imprisoned, the terms of his release. Mandela strenuously, on several occasions, made it clear to Botha, and all his emissaries before, that he, Mandela, was not the African National Congress (ANC) leader—Oliver Tambo was. But as the whole world knew (as did Botha and de Klerk), Mandela, by virtue of his referent and expert power, was the *de facto* leader of the ANC! By negotiating for the ANC's interests and all of South Africa's ahead of his own, Mandela empowered not only the ANC, but all South Africans, even though it involved rejecting de Klerk's offer of his early release, which would have been unfavorable for the ANC and South Africa. Mandela, despite knowing he had both the Botha and de

31. 1 Cor 12:26.

32. Exod 18:17–18.

Klerk regimes on the defense, did not let power go to his head, or become drunk therewith; neither attitude is characteristic of a leader who empowers others. Mandela had no problem relinquishing his enormous power to his subordinates; neither did he become president for life or die in office, both of which he could easily have done. Mandela's postures, values, and track record, before and during imprisonment, contributed to empowering the ANC and South Africa long before his release, because Mandela, back then, gave his "people the knowledge . . . self-awareness, authority, freedom . . . and opportunity to manage themselves."[33]

There are, however, obstacles that get in the way of empowerment. Gill identifies among them "a bureaucratic culture that emphasizes maintenance of the *status quo* and impedes change . . . and personal time constraints due to workload."[34] He elaborates further that "barriers to empowerment include bureaucracy, risk aversion, the need for control over others, fear of a loss of control, a lack of trust, the skill and time required to do it, and resistance to being empowered among those receiving it due to their distrust of the motives and consequences."[35] These should be no strangers to anyone who knows churches very well; for bureaucracy, status quo, and time constraints seem to breed well in congregational and denominational organizations. There is yet another barrier that impedes empowerment, though Gill doesn't so identify it: individualism. This, too, is an enemy of the congregation, which is continually and consistently identified as one flock and one body, under one Lord, within one faith and one baptism, and which is challenged to maintain that unity.[36] As hinted at before, Gill adds that "a lack of trust is the enemy of empowerment."[37] Where trust is absent, problematic phenomena, such as suspicion, fear, doubt, and paranoia may arise. These all fly in the face of the values that congregations and Christians should cultivate, including encouragement to submit to one another out of reverence for Christ,[38] allowing love to be sincere and without hypocrisy,[39] and pursuing perfect love that eliminates fear.[40]

33. Gill, *Theory*, 216.

34. Ibid., 238.

35. Ibid., 231.

36. Eph 4:1–6.

37. Gill, *Theory*, 248.

38. Eph 5:21.

39. Rom 12:9.

40. 1 John 4:18.

David Magee catalogues a fascinating account about empowerment in Toyota Motors.[41] He relates the measures Toyota's leaders put in place that catapulted the company to be the number one car maker. One measure in particular stands out: that Toyota's managers should manage as though they had no power.[42] In the spirit of relating quality to honesty and truth,[43] Toyota encourages every worker on the assembly line to shut the whole plant down (by pulling a cord) the moment a problem is caught. That way, everyone knows the problem, learns from it, and is invested in correcting it. Toyota's bosses gave workers the authority to speak truth to power; so any ordinary assembly line worker could take the initiative to shut the whole powerful Toyota plant down! That a worker, at the lowest level, could make this decision, and that management, at the highest level, would be prepared to learn from this, is the quintessence of empowerment. Toyota's leaders empower all middle managers and their employees, to "go beyond what they are told and be creative, building quality into the process."[44] Toyota's top management was told to "act not as a boss but as a facilitator."[45] The exact antithesis of this empowerment culture was found also within the motor industry during the very years that Toyota was number one: Ford Motors. While Toyota was becoming number one, Ford was losing billions of dollars. Ford's workers were being commanded to do what they were told, no questions asked. This killed worker initiative, creativity, joy, and power. This was not the first time, either, that this kind of leadership culture existed at Ford. Maxwell relates the story of how Henry Ford, later in his life and career, became eccentric and controlling, and how significant losses for the company followed.[46] There may be significance of a cultural kind, in the fact that one of these companies has a Japanese ethos and the other, an American; for eastern and western cultures and attitudes differ, each producing different leadership dynamics.

Gill refers to an even more interesting Brazilian company which he calls the "epitome of empowerment."[47] In that company, "employees choose their

41. Magee, *Toyota.*
42. Ibid., chapter 13.
43. Ibid., chapter 5.
44. Ibid., 173.
45. Ibid., 177–78.
46. Maxwell, *21 Laws,* 122–3.
47. Gill, *Theory,* 240.

managers; decide their pay . . . decide when they work: meetings are voluntary . . . the company . . . is 'out of control,'"[48] but quite successful!

By now, the benefits of empowerment should be evident. Gill sums up the benefits in this one sentence: "Sharing power does not diminish power; in fact sharing power multiplies power."[49] Regarding the church, the gift of God's power in the Holy Spirit was delivered to every believer at Pentecost. That enables all believers to join together in unleashing that power in their various tasks, energies, and services, which are all, however, a singular work and ministry. Church leaders who appreciate this truth would welcome empowerment to their organizations.

TRANSFORMATIONAL LEADERSHIP

Leadership that transforms congregations must be transformational leadership. Northouse summarizes transformational leadership as "a process that changes and transforms people. It is concerned with emotions, values, ethics, standards, and long-term goals. It includes assessing followers' motives, satisfying their needs, and treating them as full human beings. Transformational leadership involves an exceptional form of influence that moves followers to accomplish more than what is usually expected of them. It is a process that often incorporates charismatic and visionary leadership."[50]

CULTURAL SENSITIVITY

Even though globalization appears to be experiencing resistance, attack, and even reversal, and even though governments may clamp down on illegal immigration, the global exchange and movement of peoples across cultural boundaries is not going to cease anytime soon. Even what used to be considered homogeneous societies are now being understood as multicultural, even though some of these may in fact be subcultures. Cultural literacy is absolutely necessary for effective leadership; this does not apply only to "melting-pots" such as New York City or Los Angeles; it applies also to small town America where, in a sea of Euro-Americans, an African family from Cameroon or an Indian couple from Kolkata, show up as part of the church

48. Ibid., 241.

49. Ibid., 246.

50. Northouse, *Leadership*, 185.

community or organization. It applies to Kingston, Jamaica, where, in a sea of Kingstonians, someone from rural Mile Gully, Manchester, shows up. For the sake of effective leadership dynamics and community-building, and especially when there is a variety of cultures and one or more of them is a distinct minority, cultural learning becomes extremely important.

If an American or Swiss national working in Africa does not know the saying, "God gave the African time, and the Westerner a watch"[51] or does not know what it means, there are likely to be issues for the leader, whether he is the Westerner or African. Cultural sensitivity is more than just being aware of diversity; and diversity awareness goes much further than accommodating the other, integrating with the other, or even warmly and generously recognizing the other. It goes to—and beyond—*celebrating* the other, as well as our own selves in the other, until we are the other and the others are we. It is what Africans call *ubuntu*: a "humaneness—a pervasive spirit of caring and community, harmony and hospitality, respect and responsiveness—that individuals and groups display for one another."[52] Ubuntu value flies in the face of the rugged individualism that governs and infiltrates the global north and west and creates problems for leadership relationships in community. Ubuntu suggests that we cannot see ourselves until we see others; it means that I cannot be me until I see you.[53] African and Asian customs rely heavily on deference to others, primarily on the basis of age. This is somewhat foreign to the global north and west. However, deference to persons on the basis of age—despite its many values—may be somewhat problematic, not only in the north but in the south as well. This is so because it may perpetuate the entrenchment of the potentially harmful idea of hierarchy in leadership, which is a barrier to empowerment anywhere.

Still, Asian and African cultures which balk against rugged individualism encourage the idea that leadership is not effective until each participant in a community or organization recognizes one another as a *person*, and all as equally valid and valuable. In her reflections on Lao Tsu and Confucius, Kellerman observes an Eastern value in which "wise rulers never oblige the ruled to do anything."[54] This culture affirms that leaders and followers are equals. Companies and organizations that embrace this insight, even if not the culture (such as Toyota, arguably as much American, now, as

51. Mangaliso, "Building Competitive Advantage," 28.

52. Ibid., 24.

53. See Kritzinger, "Question of Missions."

54. Kellerman, *Leadership*, 8.

it is Asian), even if they experienced a difficult learning curve, should do well. Congregational and church organizations who subscribe to the idea of mutual submission of each to the other, with no distinction between leader and follower, and whose founder and leader has modeled this value very well, should be foremost among the world's organizations that model this, and extol its power and virtues.

SERVANT LEADERSHIP

The academic world may have sat up when Greenleaf introduced the idea of servant leadership.[55] But every church person knows that centuries before Greenleaf, Jesus of Nazareth established, for people who would subscribe to his kingdom, the principle, value, and virtue of servant leadership. After the Zebedee brothers were presented to him by their mother as suitable (and the only) candidates for being his right and left hand men in his coming kingdom (much to the chagrin of the other ten disciples) Jesus took the opportunity to deliver a lesson on servant leadership:

> You've observed how godless rulers throw their weight around, how quickly a little power goes to their heads. It's not going to be that way with you. Whoever wants to be great must become a servant. Whoever wants to be first among you must be your slave. That is what the Son of Man has done: He came to serve, not be served—and then to give away his life in exchange for the many who are held hostage.[56]

One clear reason congregations are warned against choosing novices in the faith for leadership in the church[57] is that the very call to follow Jesus Christ is a call to be servant. After all, "it's impossible for anyone to learn how to be a good leader without at the same time learning how to be a good follower."[58] The assumption is that, by the time a member is selected for some leadership responsibility, he would have been sufficiently steeped in the virtue and practice of serving; and it would be as much his long record of service and his attitude of serving, as his skills and abilities, that should be considered qualifications for leading. Congregational and denominational

55. Greenleaf, *Servant*.
56. Matt 20:25–28 (The Message Version).
57. 1 Tim 3:6, 10; 5:22.
58. Kellerman, "How Bad Leadership Happens," 45.

organizations and their leaders must consciously resist and desist from any semblance, idea, notion of, or attempt to associate promotion with leadership positions, especially the ordained ministry. From Jim Jones to pedophile pastors and priests, and from established denominations to televangelists, there is a plethora of evidence of what goes horribly wrong when congregational and denominational leaders stop being servants and start being lords and rulers. But much of what goes wrong never hits the airwaves or becomes public scandals; instead, the wrong is evident in sick congregations, stifled ministries, and inefficient churches and denominational organizations. Therein, members know something is wrong; they often know the source or cause of the wrong, and yet either lack the will, the power, or the skills to address it. When, in church organizations, servant leadership begins to disappear, they have begun their journey, courtesy of their (often seemingly untouchable) leaders, towards dysfunction.

TOXIC LEADERSHIP

Reducing or removing servant attitudes from leadership not only leads a church into dysfunction; it first contributes to making the leader and leadership dynamics toxic. Despite all of the foregoing leadership recommendations, leaders and leadership can go wrong in a hurry. This may be due to a variety of reasons, ranging from mismatch, to carelessness, to incompetence. But sometimes leaders and leadership go wrong because of badness, malice, narcissistic self-serving, and deliberate unprofessionalism. This is known as toxic leadership.

Kellerman makes the excellent point that "we can no more promote good leadership without studying the pathogenesis of bad leadership than we can promote strong, sturdy bodies without studying the diseases that disable and fell them."[59] Kellerman makes the distinction between leadership that is "bad as in *ineffective* and bad as in *unethical*."[60] It is the latter with which we concern ourselves here. In her continuum of seven descriptors of bad leadership ranging from ineffective to unethical, it is for the reader to determine where unethical begins: from incompetent, to rigid, to intemperate, to callous, to corrupt, to insular, then to evil, leadership.[61]

59. Ibid., 41.
60. Ibid., 43.
61. Ibid., 43–44.

- The callous leader, as well as some of the organization's members, cares about self, and nothing about the members of the organization.

- Corrupt leaders, as well as some of the organization's members, "lie, cheat, or steal."[62]

- Insular leaders, as well as some of the organization's members, "minimize or disregard the health and welfare" of others.

- Evil leaders, as well as some of the organization's members, "commit atrocities . . . use pain as an instrument of power . . . harm men, women, and children . . . and it can be physical, psychological, or both."[63]

This would be awful enough in business, politics, government, or the military; but it is infinitely worse and iniquitous when it happens—as it certainly does—in church and religious organizations. What is worse is that often, in many such organizations, the members notice, recognize, feel, and even suffer under and from this evil and toxicity; yet they seem either disinterested in or unable to do anything about it. Perhaps this may be so because the "individual toxic leader does not necessarily operate in toxic mode in all situations, nor all of the time even in the same circumstances."[64]

A toxic leader may be among the most charming of personalities, yet the most narcissistic; he may be full of flattery for others, yet devoid of actions toward them that validate those sentiments. He may appear generous to a chosen few, but is mean toward others. From many of those to whom he appears generous, he is really seeking payback and favors. He twists, or is economical with, the truth, or lies outright. He retains power at all costs. He puts down others in order to either feel good about himself, or to elevate himself in their eyes. He keeps all competitors (even if they are imaginary ones) at bay. He is far more interested in his own upward mobility than he is in the true health of his organization, and does enough to keep the organization reasonably afloat; yet he is either oblivious to or unconcerned with the failing health of the organization. He thrives in an organization where there is a woeful measure of incompetence or impotence or apathy, where his colleagues, associates or even his board are either afraid to, or otherwise disinterested in, bringing him to accountability. In many cases, they may have tried, lamely, but lost energy, will, or steam. Because the organization doesn't appear to be falling apart, and because the leader's convenient

62. Ibid., 44.

63. Ibid.

64. Lipman-Blumen, "Allure," 1.

charm and political skills serve him well, the organization tolerates the toxicity. This is part of the dishonesty of (and in) organizations to which Bolman and Deal refer.

Lipman-Blumen asks a series of important questions; even before the answers come, the questions alert us to the insidiousness and extent of toxic leadership within organizations. The questions all locate responsibility for toxic leadership squarely on the shoulders of membership who "not only tolerate, but so often prefer, and sometimes even create toxic leaders . . . [in] religious institutions."[65] She asserts that we even *want* toxic leaders and are attracted to them![66] For example, "we frequently fail to distinguish between the *noble visions* of non-toxic leaders and the *grand illusions* of their toxic counterparts."[67]

Church people—who describe their beloved leaders with accolades ranging from dynamic, to charismatic, to anointed, should sit up and heed the warning of leadership scholars who "reviewed the dark side of charismatic leaders: narcissism, authoritarianism, Machiavellianism, flawed vision, a need for power coupled with a lack of activity."[68] Some other leadership scholars point to the thin line between the virtues of a transformational leader and the vices of what they call the pseudo-transformational leader: some, like Martin, Sims, and Bailey hold that "to succeed, all leaders must be manipulative."[69] However, Bass and Steidlmeier assert that "in fact, it is pseudo-transformational leaders who are deceptive and manipulative. Authentic transformational leaders may have to be manipulative at times for what they judge to be the common good, but manipulation is a frequent practice of pseudo-transformational leaders and an infrequent practice of authentic transformational leaders."[70]

As Kellerman and Lipman-Blumen allude, there is a point beyond which toxic leaders become simply evil. Often, the toxicity is as petty as it is evil. It is the experience which Edward Dixon remembers well. Dixon's denomination had never before, in its one hundred sixty-five years of existence, placed new pastors under a probationary period. In Dixon's churches, it was his denomination—not individual churches—who approved and ordained

---

65. Ibid.
66. Ibid., 2.
67. Ibid (emphases hers).
68. Bass and Steidlmeier, "Ethics," 182.
69. Ibid.
70. Ibid.

pastors. Until this time, approval for ordination constituted either graduation from seminary, or acclamation by a congregation that one of their own (usually a deacon who had served long and well) was ready for ordination. Two years before Dixon graduated from seminary, one of his colleagues, who had struggled academically, was the catalyst for the Evergreen Fellowship—Dixon's churches—to institute a probationary system. Men, who were ordained the moment they came home from seminary, were now presiding over a probationary process, which was meant to last two years. Dixon's colleague came through the probationary period just fine, and was ordained.

When Dixon arrived back home in Evergreen, fresh from seminary, he was placed, as expected, and in accordance with the Fellowship's polity, on probation. Dixon was never given any guidelines or metrics or presented with any requirements he had to fulfill during this probationary period. He was assigned a supervisor, with whom he had a good relationship. This was a man with several years of pastoral service. A couple of years before Dixon's graduation from seminary, he had had an exchange of letters with some of Evergreen's leaders. A list of reasons he offered for a request for a certain summer assignment was dismissed as "a list of excuses." Dixon's indication that he thought this response insensitive and rude soured his relationship with one of the leaders who, at the time of Dixon's probation, was Evergreen's president. The president appears not to have forgotten Dixon's "effrontery." He made life unreasonably difficult for Dixon. By this time, a friendship had developed between Dixon's supervisor and the president.

When the time came for Dixon's two-year probationary period to end, he was advised that the period was being extended. He was offered no reason. However, in a meeting from which he was asked to excuse himself, he overheard the reason, offered to a person who questioned why Dixon was being made to undergo an extended probationary period. The reason offered by the president was: "Pastor Dixon did not have sufficient supervision." Knowing that no probationer-supervisee is expected to supervise himself, and knowing that Dixon's supervisor was one of Evergreen's senior leaders, no one challenged the injustice inherent in making Dixon responsible for his supervisor's failure to supervise him! Incredibly, the meeting approved the extension of Dixon's probation; and even more incredibly, the extension was not a few months or a year—it was two more years! Dixon progressed through those extra two years, again, with no list of requirements, no metrics, and no supervision different from what he had been offered before. It was clear to him and to others that his experience was purely the abuse of power by two people who delivered him into evil. As Dixon reflects on his ministry over the many years since, he agrees that this incident, so early in his ministry, stunted his self-confidence, underdeveloped his self-esteem, and robbed him of certain opportunities. He considers that episode as life-changing, having never expected that level of evil in church leadership.

Combating toxic leaders

Church people and members of religious organizations should never forget that bad leaders "cannot do harm without followers who enable them."[71] For toxic leadership does not reside only in those who are called leaders, but also in followers. Church folk would do well to recall the reality that toxic leaders arise because the membership *allows* them to arise, grow, and flourish! Strategies to check and then combat the proliferation of toxicity within their organizations would serve them very well. That an entire group of intelligent people sat in a meeting and never questioned Evergreen's president and Edward Dixon's pastoral supervisor about the injustice they were delivering to the young man, or challenged their placing the blame where it was unjustly due, or called out the ruse, is ample evidence of the fact that it is members who create the leadership monsters and toxic leaders they harbor. Both Kellerman and Lipman-Blumen offer some useful suggestions that congregational and denominational entities should consider.

1. From Lipman-Blumen: members should "*investigate* the toxic leader's history."[72] They should not hesitate to publish their findings among their community,[73] not so much to indecently expose the leader but to inform the community about any remaining "hopes that the leader will change."[74]

2. Next, they might "create a coalition"[75] for constructive confrontation[76] which would involve respectful engagement with the leader, which focuses more on the negative organizational impact of the leader's toxicity

---

71. Kellerman, "How Bad Leadership Happens", 45.
72. Lipman-Blumen, "Allure," 5 (emphases hers).
73. Ibid, 6.
74. Ibid.
75. Ibid.
76. Ibid.

rather than on the leader as a villain. However, Lipman-Blumen warns, tougher measures may be necessary if none of these work.

3. The organization may need to resort to measures such as "[creating] a strategy for undermining our ousting the leader."[77]

4. The organization may even consider engaging the media to finally expose the leader if nothing else works.[78] Few organizations—especially religious ones—desire the scandals risked in going that far; so hopefully, they would pursue other options, and in a timely fashion, before the mess is too big to tackle.

5. Both Lipman-Blumen and Kellerman recommend term limits;[79] in fact, it is Kellerman's first suggestion for leaders.[80]

6. Kellerman urges leaders to share power, remain honest and realistic, especially about their weaknesses and limitations, and to remain balanced and reflective.[81]

7. Members, on the other hand, should "empower . . . themselves . . . be loyal to the whole and not to any single individual . . . be skeptical [because] leaders are not gods . . . be a watchdog [because] ignorance is not bliss . . . take a stand [because] pliant board, craven aides, scared subordinates, submissive underlings, and passive bystanders are as much to blame for bad leadership as are bad leaders . . . [and] find allies [because] in numbers there is strength."[82]

Jerome Roberts was called to be pastor of the Springhill Baptist Church. However, after the death of the search committee's chairman, the committee went rogue. Even though Roberts received a near unanimous vote from the congregation, certain members of the search committee had their own agenda. Letters to the congregation from Roberts were all intercepted by the search committee, including ones requesting to meet with the congregation that had just voted to call him. The search committee replied to Roberts, ostensibly on behalf of the congregation who never saw Roberts's letters. The two members of the search committee who had no ill-will toward Roberts

77. Ibid.
78. Ibid.
79. Ibid.
80. Kellerman, "How Bad Leadership Happens," 45.
81. Ibid.
82. Ibid.

were timid and powerless to challenge the other seven who did. Some members of the congregation also knew of the search committee's shenanigans. But no one did anything to stop them. Roberts appealed to persons within and without the congregation, and to church executives of his denomination to intervene and bring some fairness and justice to the process. One of them counseled and encouraged Roberts, but nobody acted.

Finally, after months of obfuscation and obstructionism, the search committee simply presented another candidate to the church. The church, without as much as a question about the process (or based on lies they were told about Roberts), voted, and called its next pastor—all this without even a letter to Roberts, indicating that this was being done. This was a classic case of bad leadership that was allowed to take root and hurt people, while the knowing membership simply stood by and did nothing. Even if Springhill's progress since were not conflicted and troubled—which it still is, decades later—it would still be true to say that here was a congregation that was led into dysfunction—or allowed itself to be so led.

Church institutions thrive on good leadership. Any signs of bad leadership should be attended to, and dealt with urgently and thoroughly, taking care, always, to protect the fragility of the flock, wherever and whenever the wolf of bad leadership appears.

Chapter 8

George Liele: Transformational Pastor and Missionary

AMONG THE CARIBBEAN ISLANDS and territories, Baptist witness has enjoyed the most favorable passage and thrived best in Jamaica. Between 2007 and 2017, a Jamaican was general secretary of the Baptist World Alliance, while its associate director for communications is also Jamaican. The Alliance is the official organization of the world's 41.5 million Baptists. Three of Jamaica's six National Heroes were Baptists. Not every Jamaican Baptist would say that Baptist witness has exercised its best efforts or achieved its highest goals; but that issue is for a different book (though it might be said that perhaps some of the reasons and remedies for that might both be found in some of the chapters in this book).

Adoniram and Ann Judson are celebrated as the first Christian missionaries ever to leave the United States for foreign soil. However, three decades before the Judsons departed for Burma, George Liele, a former slave, sailed from Savannah, Georgia, for Jamaica. This was also a decade before William Carey left the eastern edge of the Atlantic for India. It is to George Liele that Jamaican Baptists owe their origins. From all the records available, Liele was a remarkable leader. Only a few publications exist about Liele as a missionary, a pioneer, a slave, a soldier, a church planter, and a pastor. In perhaps the earliest study on him, Clement Gayle declares that "it is almost as if there has been a conspiracy to ignore Liele"[1]—this, perhaps because there are volumes written about the Judsons and Carey, and others who came after them. After all, nothing momentous or even pioneering could be expected in those times, to come from a former slave or a black

1. Gayle, *Liele*, unnumbered preface page.

90

man. Indeed, it is only within the last decade that the American Baptist Churches came to recognize and celebrate Liele as the first missionary from America. Even now, that remains somewhat unofficial; the Judsons still retain the formal slot.[2] Gayle's sketch of Liele is biographical and historical in nature. But what about George Liele as a leader? There lies a treasure-trove of leadership insights in this man who lived, led, and died so long ago.

BIOGRAPHICAL OVERVIEW

When George Liele arrived in Jamaica in 1783, he was already a leader. Liele is never found dithering about whether it was time he took up the mantle of leadership. From the moment he is converted to Christianity, Liele appears to knowingly take up that mantle, though not in any grabbing, grasping, or power-snatching sense. Born a slave in Virginia around 1750, George Liele's family, fortunate to escape the separation many slaves endured, were nevertheless exposed to moving several times, finally ending up in Georgia. Perhaps what helped to keep the family together was his family's master, Henry Sharp, who was a deacon in the Baptist church in Georgia. Liele was therefore exposed to the Christian faith from an early age.

From the time Liele was converted to Christianity in 1773, he had a sense of call and a sense of leadership. Regarding his conversion experience, Liele wrote, "I requested of my Lord and Master to give me a work. I did not care how mean it was, only to try and see how good I would do it."[3] Liele was licensed to preach that very same year and, remarkably, founded his first, second, and perhaps, even third church that very same year! All this took place before Liele was even ordained a minister; that happened two years later, in 1775! Liele was the first Black person ever to be ordained as a Christian minister in the United States.

The "First African Baptist Church was organized in 1773 under the leadership of Reverend George Leile [sic]."[4] First African, as well as First Bryan Baptist, both in Georgia, lay claim to Liele as their founder. A third, which did not survive due to the outbreak of the American Revolutionary War, tends to be forgotten. This one was in Silver Bluff, Georgia.[5] These three churches are the first black churches ever to be established in the

2. International Ministries, "Past, Present and Future," lines 4–5.
3. Ibid., 7.
4. First African Baptist Church, "First African," line 2.
5. Gayle, *Liele*, 8.

United States, all of them started by George Liele; and two of them still stand today. Liele's leadership prowess is evident long before he arrives in Jamaica.

The American Revolutionary War (1775–1783) was impactful not only on America, not only on England, but also on Jamaica, and the Caribbean as a whole. The British promised American slaves their freedom if they fought for them; this incentive drew many slaves into the British army. Everyone now knows that the British lost, and therefore had to leave America. As the British left, companies of former slave-soldiers left America with them for various parts of the Caribbean, in order to obtain their promised freedom. There remain even now, several villages in Trinidad and Tobago, actually named Third Company, Fourth Company, Fifth Company, and Sixth Company, named after the particular group of soldiers that landed and settled there after the war.

In 1782, George Liele, having fought for the British, set sail for Jamaica with a batch of British soldiers. Gayle suggests that, British promise aside, what may have precipitated Liele's departure was a brief imprisonment at the behest of his slave-master's family and the threat of re-enslavement.[6] A British colonel named Kirkland, destined for Jamaica, bought Liele's freedom and loaned him the money for his family's passage to Jamaica. Thus, this former slave—now indentured laborer, Baptist pastor, evangelist, and leader, with two historical "firsts" to his name—arrived in Jamaica in 1783 with his family, where he would score the third, fourth, fifth, and sixth "firsts": he would be the first Baptist on Jamaican soil who was not white; the first black preacher ever on the island; the first black preacher ever to preach exclusively to blacks in Jamaica; and the first black man ever to establish a church in Jamaica.

In Jamaica, Liele would fortuitously land a job with the governor of Jamaica, who was a friend of Colonel Kirkland's. This work enabled Liele to repay his loan to Kirkland and secure his freedom, at least fifty years before emancipation was proclaimed in Jamaica. The measure of brutality to which Jamaican slaves were exposed was considered far worse than what Liele had ever seen in America.[7] For example, *lynching*—that awful, brutal and inhumane hate-crime unleashed upon blacks in the American south— is said to have been created in Jamaica by Charles and William Lynch, and then exported to America. Though a free man, this must have made an

6. Ibid., 11.
7. Ibid., 1.

indelible impression on Liele, and must have found easy fusion with his sense of purpose and vision for leadership, already formed and continuing to strengthen. As Gayle asserts, "things were ripe for change."[8] This should not lead one however, to measure Liele by the *great man* leadership theory, no matter how tempting.

Not long after his arrival in Jamaica, Liele meets Moses Baker, a former slave from New York. Baker becomes a Christian convert, and Liele baptizes him. Shortly thereafter, Liele, based in Kingston, commissions Baker to Montego Bay, on the other end of the island, to preach and baptize there. This is a significantly strategic move that demonstrates Liele's dedication to his vision, as well as his intelligence. Among the several hundred other converts Liele baptizes are Nicholas Thomas Sweigle and George Gibbs. Liele nurtures, mentors, and develops these three men, who in turn help Liele develop the work of evangelism, liberation, and Baptist witness on the island.

Sometime around 1793, Liele is imprisoned (one of many such experiences), despite being a free man. On this occasion, he had previously secured a loan for church-building purposes and, when his poor congregation (made up of slaves and free, yet poor, blacks) was unable to repay the loan, Liele was imprisoned. During this time, he left his son, Paul, in charge of the church—not Deacon Sweigle. This may have been a catalyst for problems that led to Sweigle and Liele parting company after the latter's release.[9] Whether this was a case of nepotism or a response to some weakness Liele perceived in Sweigle, is not known. Sweigle's response may or may not suggest the latter; he moved on elsewhere, establishing churches and baptizing converts. He and Liele would later reconcile, somewhat.[10]

By 1814, significant marks of progress had become evident: there were eight thousand Baptist converts in six of Jamaica's fourteen parishes, including Sweigle and Baker's congregations.[11] By this time, too, Liele had made contact with William Wilberforce, the British emancipator, through Methodist connections in Jamaica. Liele and Baker (with some inducement) made sufficient contact with British Baptists so as to result in their sending the first British Baptist missionary to Jamaica.[12] The relationship between the British and Jamaican Baptists continues fraternally to this

---

8. Ibid., 2.

9. Russell, *Baptist Witness*, 111; Gayle, *Liele*, 18–19.

10. Gayle, *Liele*, 24.

11. Ibid., 33.

12. Russell, *Baptist Witness*, 112–13.

day—the formal missionary-sending partnership ending as recently as the first decade of the twenty-first century.

By the time the emancipation proclamation is read in Spanish Town, Jamaica, in 1838, George Liele had been dead for less than a decade. Nevertheless, during the George Liele years, "Baptists declared themselves on the side of the poor and oppressed sons and daughters of Africa."[13] This is only a small part of the legacy Liele has left Jamaica.

GEORGE LIELE—THE TRANSFORMATIONAL AUTHENTIC

George Liele's impact on the people he met in general and on the people of Jamaica in particular is nothing short of transformational. As a person and leader he was authentic, not just in the ordinary sense of the word, but in the way leadership theory understands the word *authentic*. In leadership theory, authenticity refers to the unique character, strength, and leadership acumen that reposes in an individual, all of which result from crucial, even epochal, life events that shape the individual. George Liele's life story demonstrates beyond any doubt, the source of his authenticity—an authenticity so firmly, clearly and indelibly etched on him, inside out. Because of this dual nature of George Liele—his transforming impact on people, on history and on Jamaica, and his authenticity—we define, describe, and declare George Liele to be a transformational and authentic leader. More than that, we omit the label of *leader*, so as to communicate that Liele, such an epitome of authenticity, should simply be designated *the transformational authentic*, where authentic is a noun, not an adjective. Undergirding this position of the transformational authentic is a handful of leadership issues, concepts, and observations that we shall explore in due course.

A DEFINITION OF LEADERSHIP

Leadership definitions abound; it may therefore seem superfluous or unnecessary to add one more to the labyrinth. But when one takes a look at George Liele, a new definition of leadership emerges. As with every other leadership definition, this one is certainly neither exhaustive nor comprehensive. It can be said that definitions of leadership are really constructs—perspectives—of the student, scholar, researcher, or observer, at a given point in time,

13. Gayle, *Liele*, 35.

depending on the context in which leadership issues are being considered. Leadership *theories*, as stated before, are quite fluid and dynamic; so too, are leadership *definitions*. Consider this author's definition of leadership: Leadership is the process by which two or more persons become engaged in a mutual and purposeful relationship; they encourage and facilitate one another to achieve the purposeful and compelling goals and vision of that relationship. This happens when at least one person's vision, conviction, intelligence, and skills all combine to keep him/her and the others focused on the values and purpose underlying those goals and that vision.

This definition certainly exceeds the position that "leadership is influence—nothing more, nothing less."[14] That position does not identify who influences whom, why, or how. Kellerman does nearly the same: "As I define it, a *leader* chooses a particular course of action and then in some way gets others to go along, or, more subtly, the leader encourages the led to 'choose' the course that the group will follow."[15] While she identifies who influences whom, she only vaguely hints at how, and says nothing about why. Both Maxwell and Kellerman—competent leadership practitioner, and competent leadership academic respectively—demonstrate the sheer difficulty of constructing a definition of leadership devoid of inadequacies. Doubtlessly, the one offered here, even if inspired by one as great as George Liele, is likely to be found inadequate by someone else who comes from a different context and with a different perspective. Nevertheless, the definition is an attempt at an apt and adequate description of George Liele, the transformational authentic, and by extension, leaders who are transformational and authentic. It offers to the leadership student and practitioner, another rung in the ladder toward a fuller understanding of this phenomenon called leadership.

THE TRANSFORMATIONAL AUTHENTIC LEADER—OVERVIEW

The Transformational Authentic is a seamless combination of transformational leadership, authenticity, authentic leadership, and an empowering *modus operandi,* all of which are supported with and informed by a cluster of leadership intelligences. This model is described in Figure 1. In a single person—George Liele, in this case—all of these components are housed harmoniously, and he/she is more than the sum total of all these.

14. Maxwell, *21 Laws,* 17.

15. Kellerman, *Bad Leadership,* xiii, emphasis hers.

The Transformational Authentic — the Four Components

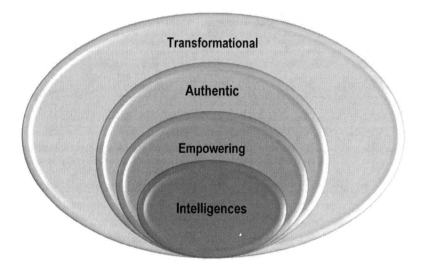

Figure 1

The transformational authentic is a transformational leader

George Liele made history. He "was a pioneer . . . he was not just the first Baptist, or the first black minister to preach in Jamaica, but the first one to win a significant number of slaves on the Island to Christ . . . the first to organize a church made up predominantly of negroes on the Island."[16] Were Liele viewed as a transformer only from the perspective of either changing history, or making history, that in itself would be significant. However, Liele was a transformational leader also from a leadership theory viewpoint, which addresses character and competencies—not just happenings, or happenstance, or history. There are two current Jamaican realities for which Liele is credited: starting "one of Jamaica's strongest Protestant denominations"[17] and doing groundbreaking work in the field of education.[18] Since public education in Jamaica is still significantly joined at the

16. Gayle, *Liele*, 3.
17. Ibid., 35.
18. Ibid., 39.

hip with the churches, and since not a few of Jamaica's leaders (as well as some notable ones of Jamaican birth or ancestry beyond Jamaica's shores) hail from both Jamaica's churches and schools, many effective Jamaican and international leaders should lay claim to George Liele's legacy, at least in part. Avolio and Bass observe that "true transformational leaders . . . convert their followers into leaders."[19] The records show that George Liele did precisely this with Moses Baker, George Gibbs, Thomas Sweigle, and countless others of his flock. Jamaica's Baptists, as well as the wider Jamaican church, have carried on this legacy to the present.

We asked before whose expectations and what metrics Northouse was referencing in his affirmation that transformational leadership gets out of people "more than what is usually expected" of them.[20] Perhaps Northouse was channeling Avolio and Bass; perhaps not. The latter two are ambiguous about whether the expectations repose in the followers or in the leaders: "*Transformational* leaders motivate others to do more than they originally intended and often even more than they thought possible."[21] One is uncertain whether the word *they* refers to the leaders or the followers either of the two times it is used; it could conceivably be either. Whether or not it is the leaders whose expectations are exceeded, it would have to be concluded that the followers would have been so motivated and empowered as to deliver results that exceed somebody's expectations. Either way, this affirms the position that a transformational leader is an empowering leader.

All that said, by the (European and colonial) world's expectations of the time, certain feats would never have been expected of black people, let alone slaves: preaching, ordination, pioneering, church-planting, church-growing, denomination-starting, lay-people training, pastoral development, school-starting, and more. George Liele stands among the rare handful of non-Europeans of that era who exceeded those expectations. With Liele in mind, transformational leadership might be described as that leadership which ignites people to move beyond previous limits—whether those limits were their own, or others'—and, when they have done that, to motivate them to do it again, going even further, the next time. This is what Liele appeared able to do with the people who fell within the ambit of his leadership.

Transformational leadership, whatever the definition, tends to either state or imply mutual motivation and encouragement of both leader and

19. Avolio and Bass, *Developing Potential*, 1.

20. Northouse, *Leadership*, 171.

21. Avolio and Bass, *Developing Potential*, 1, emphasis theirs.

follower, initiated by the leader toward—as is often stated or implied—action that exceeds somebody's expectations. In Figure 2, which represents the transformational component of George Liele's transformational authentic profile, this mutuality is captured. If there are eight thousand Baptist converts on the island by 1814,[22] Figure 2 suggests that by Liele's death, probably about fifteen years later, it is likely that there were twelve thousand slaves or former slaves who have become the Baptists of Jamaica![23] These are the products of Liele and his motivated and empowered protégés. These are the people who would—empowered and emboldened by both Liele's example and the gospel they believed—eventually fight for and secure emancipation from slavery.[24]

Transformational Authentic Leadership — the Transformational Component

Transformational:

Leader and followers are **motivator** and **motivated**: Liele motivates **12,000** slaves to salvation, church-pioneering, and emancipation; they motivate him to serve; **this is transformational leadership.**

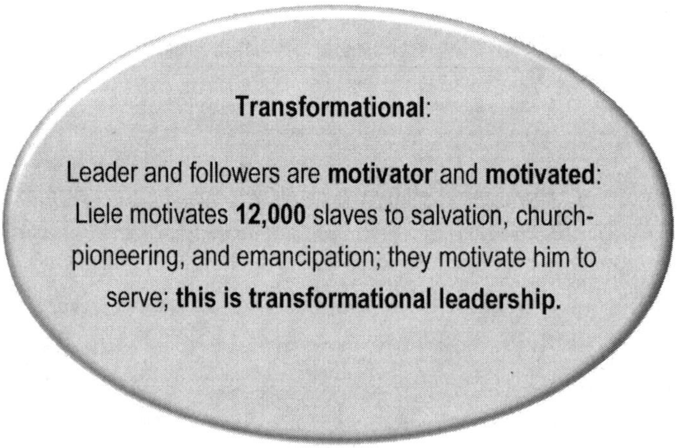

Figure 2

---

22. Gayle, *Liele*, 33.

23. This is possible if the movement maintained, for the next fifteen years, the same rate of growth it saw in the first twenty-nine years.

24. The 1831–1832 uprising in Jamaica (December 25, 1831—January 4, 1832), led by Sam Sharpe, enlisted more than sixty thousand of the island's three hundred thousand slaves. Although those who joined the uprising were Sharpe's followers, it is unclear how many were Baptists, and direct or "descendant" converts of Liele's.

Transformational factors in George Liele's leadership

As previously indicated, leadership authorities and experts all agree that there are four key components of transformational leadership, usually referred to as the 4 I's: *idealized influence, inspirational motivation, intellectual stimulation,* and *individualized consideration.*

IDEALIZED INFLUENCE

Idealized influence is otherwise called charisma, because it involves the leader's displayed and genuine interest in the followers. This interest is communicated through genuine (authentic) care, listening, and empathy. The followers, in turn, give the leader respect, and, in viewing him/her as the ideal leader, they are induced to give respect, trust, and cooperation. Transformational leaders "talk about . . . values, beliefs, purposes, a collective mission, and the benefits of trusting each other."[25] Buoyed by the high calling of salvation in and service to Christ, Liele would have preached and ministered with these qualities. He had no incentive or reward to give anyone for following him, so theirs could not be what leadership theory refers to in those circumstances, as a transactional leadership relationship (defined by rewards from leader to follower to induce following). Neither did they have any reward to offer Liele—he worked as a minister for no pay.

Perhaps the novelty of hearing the gospel preached, or seeing benevolent leadership being practiced by a black man, might have contributed significantly to Liele's charisma and credibility. This touches on aspects of authenticity, the seamless partner of transformational leadership.

INSPIRATIONAL MOTIVATION

Liele is an excellent model of *inspirational motivation.* To his followers, Liele embodied ideally in himself, even if subliminally, what his followers could become as black people: free, saved (as in Christ's salvation) and leaders. They could see in Liele that which he was calling them to follow. Contemporary leaders should examine how they can embody, with all authenticity, that to which they seek to lead people. It is for the reader to determine whether some preachers who live in opulence (usually derived from their followers who are far less affluent than they), who come preaching material

25. Sosik and Jung, *Full-Range Leadership,* 15.

prosperity, are the embodiment of authenticity or inspirational motivation. It is for the reader to determine whether those preachers' means, ends, theology, techniques, and lifestyles qualify them as authentic, or whether they might be the epitome of whom Avolio and Bass define as pseudo-transformational leaders, who "are . . . self-aggrandizing, exploitative and narcissistic."[26] The deception is complete when the poor victims who fall for such preachers' doctrines think they are being *inspired* and *motivated,* while in fact they are ceding their wealth, time, and hope to these charlatans! They may think they are being empowered, when they listen to sermon after sermon on pop psychology and self-help, when instead they are being lulled into dependency, and the transfer of their wealth to a wealthier pastor. The report about Liele is far different: he "was no charlatan."[27]

INTELLECTUAL STIMULATION

Intellectual stimulation is the third pillar of transformational leadership. Gayle provides one singularly crucial piece of information that gives insight into George Liele's prowess in this quality. We made reference earlier to Liele's numerous convictions and imprisonment. "On one occasion he was charged with sedition after preaching a sermon on Romans 10:1 in which he expressed a strong desire for freedom from sin and its consequences."[28] Without the script of that sermon, one is left to speculate about what it was that earned Liele the charge of sedition. Was it that Liele viewed the British as the Israelites whom Paul earnestly desired, in the biblical verse, to be saved? Did Liele name slave masters or the plantocracy as the collective evil from which the slaves needed to be saved? Or did he say that slavery was the consequence of British sin? One does not know. What we do know of transformational leaders is that "they question the *status quo.*"[29] In that regard, Liele appears to be the quintessential transformational leader. It is worthy of investigation to see how much Liele's theology, preaching, and utterances had to do with the 1865 Baptist War in Jamaica, which took place less than a decade after Liele's death. How much did George Liele, former sedition convict, intellectually influence a slave rebellion in the name of freedom?

26. Avolio and Bass, *Developing Potential,* 9.
27. Gayle, *Liele,* 41.
28. Ibid., 17.
29. Gill, *Theory,* 84.

INDIVIDUALIZED CONSIDERATION

The fourth "I" of transformational leadership is *individualized consideration.* There is insufficient information to measure exactly how much and how closely Liele worked individually, with his parishioner-followers. As pastor of more than one congregation, and as itinerant preacher, he must have done a fair amount of "management by wandering around,"[30] giving and receiving feedback, even if it were not the same person on each visit. In those days, attending church was perhaps the only social event for slaves, and for only a few hours each opportunity; and those who could would spend at least six hours weekly in congregational meetings.[31] Perhaps many individualized relationships were forged here. After all, persuasion is done "sometimes one man at a time."[32] Liele, even if he would have persuaded or counseled persons in groups, would certainly have baptized each one at a time. He would have offered much individualized consideration to the men whom he groomed for ministry and whom he trusted with ministry in one way or another.

Authenticity factors in George Liele's leadership

George Liele was an authentic leader. In response to growing greed, corruption, and depravity in corporate America, David Gergen observes that once upon a time it was thought that "smart people were the best at most things, including leadership (but that now) what . . . distinguishes the great leaders from the mediocre are the personal, inner qualities,"[33] or an "inner compass (or) true north."[34] He adds that "authentic leaders lead with their heart as well as their heads."[35] A number of factors contribute to cultivating authenticity, many of which are observable in George Liele. Among the outstanding ones are *life experiences, purpose, vision,* and a *moral compass* or *values,* as illustrated in Figure 3. We explore these in turn as they show in Liele.

30. Ibid.
31. Gayle, *Liele*, 35.
32. Greenleaf, *Servant*, 30.
33. George, *True North*, xvii, quoting David Gergen.
34. Ibid., xx.
35. Ibid., xxxii.

Transformational Authentic Leadership — the Authentic Component

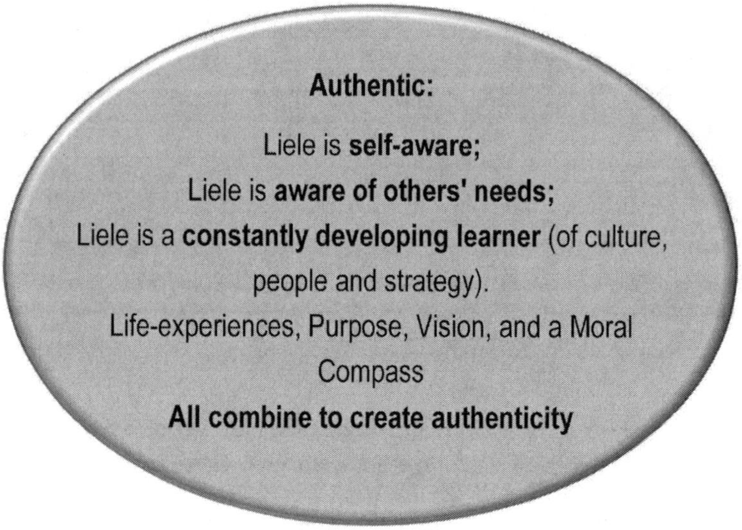

> **Authentic:**
>
> Liele is **self-aware**;
> Liele is **aware of others' needs**;
> Liele is a **constantly developing learner** (of culture,
> people and strategy).
> Life-experiences, Purpose, Vision, and a Moral
> Compass
> **All combine to create authenticity**

Figure 3

Life experiences

First, *life experiences*: Bill George writes, "Your life story defines your leadership."[36] He relates stories of a handful of Americans who, one might argue, can neither equate nor eclipse Liele's story for movement from obscurity and ordinariness to greatness—even though he includes one who moved "from cottonfields to the boardroom."[37] Emphasizing this truth, the Harvard Business Review (HBR) features seventeen leaders, including the irrepressible Jack Welch, recalling the "moments and people that shaped them."[38] Although the HBR does not actually name authenticity as the issue, it clearly recognizes and validates life experiences as among the seeds of authentic leadership that creates moments. Most of the HBR's seventeen featured leaders refer to their parents, or some hardship, or near poverty, and one, to a schoolmaster he did not even like, as the source of some significant

36. Ibid., 8.

37. Ibid., 12.

38. Collingwood, "Personal Histories," 1–23.

life experience or inspiration to which they attribute their leadership stature. One's father, in poverty, built a car out of junk. One attended a live Martin Luther King Jr. speech as a child, and another had her life-changing moment when she watched police beatings in Selma, Alabama on TV. Such are the kinds of experiences that transform people and, in turn, equip them with the seeds of authenticity to go on to transform others.

It is arguable that Liele's life experiences remain unmatched against the life experiences of these seventeen, even when the seventeen's are all taken together as one experience. Liele's multifarious experiences as a slave all weave the tapestry of authenticity—whether it was watching brutal beatings; or listening to the harrowing screams of young children being ripped from their families forever, having been sold to another plantation; or facing death as a soldier; or watching others die in battle; or as a convict (not for any crimes); or his dramatic conversion in which he cried to Jesus, "give me a work!" Due to the fact that Liele's slave-master was a Baptist, and Liele's father, "the only black person in that part of the country who knew the Lord in a 'spiritual way,'"[39] Liele was exposed to the Christian faith early in life. Consequently, he was ordained at age twenty-five, which can be considered early in many contexts today. With life experiences like these, provided one had the four I's of transformational leadership, along with leadership intelligence, one is predisposed to being a remarkable leader if opportunity arises and is embraced. The predisposition was George Liele's, and when the opportunity came his way, he grasped it.

PURPOSE

Second, *purpose*: leaders should know, and be able to articulate why, they want to lead. Authenticity "incorporates the leader's self-knowledge, self-regulation, and self-concept."[40] Leaders' purpose, discerned as they reflect on who they really are, should dovetail with the purpose of the entity or organization they lead, and it should bleed out into the way these leaders deal with their followers. This part is the *interpersonal* perspective of defining authenticity. "Why is the leader leading?" and "Why does she want us to follow her?" are two questions which, when answered, help followers know in short order whether to run as fast as they can away from their leader, throw her/him out, or rally round him/her willingly. The public secret is that followers

39. Gayle, *Liele*, 6.
40. Northouse, *Leadership*, 206.

tend to discern the answers to these questions over time, even if the leader doesn't! Gill[41] and Pearce[42] discuss authenticity with focus on what a leader says. But authenticity, before it involves what a leader says, creates the inner convictions to which the leader's speech refers and relates as its touchstone. Pearce does concede that "clarity of purpose"[43] supports communication competence—the kind that builds leader credibility and authenticity. Letters from Liele to a Dr Rippon[44] reveal Liele's elegant and sophisticated writing skills. Given his ability to influence and persuade as a preacher, he was likely well-spoken, and overall, a strong communicator. The rapid growth of Jamaican Baptist churches during Liele's first thirty years appears to attest to this, and to Liele's purpose.

The moment George Liele prayed "Give me a work" and "did not care how mean it was, only to try and see how good [he] would do it,"[45] he met his lifelong purpose from which he never swerved to the right or to the left. It was a purpose honed through slave-childhood in the cotton fields and sharpened through discipline as a soldier. "A 'good' purpose," Gill writes, "enhances the lives of those the organization serves and those who serve it and provides meaning, guidance and inspiration."[46] This is virtually a snapshot of Liele's leadership: in fulfilling the purpose of serving Jesus, he establishes Baptist witness in Jamaica, and leaves, still operating today, the first two black churches on the American continent.

As noted before, the brutality slaves experienced in Jamaica was worse than that in America. Perhaps Liele's purpose gained new energies in this new experience, even though he was not subject to that brutality himself. Perhaps this is what goaded him to preach that dangerous sermon from Romans 10:1. A leader's sense of purpose may in fact enable contingency leadership (a flexibility of response to a variety of presenting situations); and cognizance of that purpose may allow flexibility. The purpose remains constant, but the style may vary. As well, the constant purpose may not only enable, but *encourage* flexibility. "Leadership—from . . . transformational and charismatic leadership theories ˷ . is purpose driven."[47]

41. Gill, *Theory*, 280–81.

42. Pearce, *Leading Out Loud*.

43. Ibid., 70.

44. Gayle, *Liele*, 6–7, 15, 20.

45. Ibid., 7.

46. Gill, *Theory*, 136.

47. Antonakis et al., *Nature of Leadership*, 5.

VISION

Third, *vision:* Hahn describes vision as an instrument which may actually cause the visionary leader to live in a state suspended "between vision and belonging"[48] in community. Leaders who have taken stock of where their organizations are, alongside where the organizations need to be, know well this suspended state. Vision places leaders in a kind of parallel reality, the one in which they live and the one of which they dream. Visionary leaders "work in, but do not belong to, organizations."[49] Immigrants and persons who have moved either several times in their lives, or far away from the land of their birth, could, while facing obvious challenges related to this dislocation, also develop a wider perspective of life and a deeper and broader worldview. Liele, who moved several times in his life before arriving in Georgia[50] (let alone Jamaica), appears a candidate for this kind of ability to see things beyond the parochial and the immediate. He demonstrated the ability to "create disorder and excitement, and . . . change the way people think about what is possible, desirable and necessary."[51]

This matter of vision being about the future is critical; but equally important for the authentic leader is a proper vision of what the *present* is! The authentic leader has to know why the organization cannot remain where it is and why not. Knowledge of the present helps the leader understand this, especially in view of the leader's values and purpose. Heifetz and Linsky address the matter of how vision of the present is to be understood. Their image of getting on the balcony (for a panoramic view of where one is) makes their point.[52] When Liele surveyed the social landscape in Kingston, Jamaica, in 1783, remembering his request of his Lord, "give me a work" (with his central purpose being to serve the Lord) he knew what he had to do, why he had to do it, and why leaving Jamaica in the condition he found it was not going to be an option. This prepared Liele to "orchestrate the conflict"[53] so as to reach his goal. What all this does is suggest that vision is not merely seeing the future, but a *panoramic* perspective, in which *both* present and future—and what lies in between—are equally important! And

48. Hahn, *Growing in Authority,* 50.
49. Gill, *Theory,* 132.
50. Gayle, *Liele,* 6.
51. Gill, *Theory,* 132.
52. Heifetz and Linsky, *Leadership on the Line,* 51–74.
53. Ibid., 101–22.

what lies between would usually involve conflict, if only from the change-navigation that would be required to move from the present to the future.

Spears and Lawrence push the idea further, with the word *discernment*. Discernment is not exactly the same as vision; discernment informs vision, and is a precursor to vision. "Discernment arises from listening; it moves us into vision."[54] But this listening is not primarily to one's followers; it is "to be able to withdraw and listen to a wider voice, a more overarching purpose... it is to listen to God."[55] And *then,* one can add, that discernment is to hear God speaking through all the different voices in the leader-follower community. Of course, not every voice *by itself* would necessarily be God's; so even *within* the discernment process, discernment is crucial. One does not know what voices Liele heard, and how he discerned that it was God's. Often, as Jesus once said, fruits demonstrate whether a prophet was authentic or not.[56] According to the record of Jamaican Baptists, Liele's fruit speak for themselves—and for his authenticity. Liele's vision of what his work could become is what led him to be actively engaged in the process that eventually brought London's Baptist Missionary Society to Jamaica, a partnership that has resulted in the Jamaican Baptists unique growth in the Caribbean.

MORAL COMPASS

Fourth, *moral compass*: transformational authentics could not be without a moral compass. This factor is what separates them from pseudo-transformational leaders. One key test of whether a leader will be immature, bad, toxic, or evil is the leader's propensity or aversion to vindictiveness, sophistry, or lies. It should not be surprising to find "a higher level of moral reasoning . . . associated with transformational leadership."[57] Kellerman's differentiation between ineffective and unethical leadership has been noted earlier. She observes that in ineffective leadership, purposes and intentions may not be "bad" (as in morally bankrupt). Unethical leadership, however, is morally bankrupt. Ineffective leaders, though they may have morally sound purposes and intentions, may be incompetent, or rigid, or intemperate, or a poor fit for the task. Bad leaders—those with no moral compass—reveal a repertoire of callousness, corruption, insularity, and evil in

54. Spears and Lawrence, *Focus on Leadership*, 248.
55. Ibid., 249.
56. Matt 7:15–16.
57. Gill, *Theory*, 164.

their motives and purposes,[58] even though they may in fact be competent, able, and a proper fit for the task. Ethical leaders care about their followers' interests and needs; they take the high road, are self-controlled, and serve the community, not themselves. This is authenticity; this is George Liele.

There is a tragic story of two Goldman Sachs—the one in New York and the subsidiary in London.[59] It is a story of night and day. The greedy, self-consumed, intemperate, and unethical operatives in New York sullied the name, and interfered with the progress of their London office, whose staffers were the exact moral opposite of them. As investigative reports and history have both shown, the Wall Street operatives had no moral compass; this helped to nearly run the American economy aground in 2008. Equally tragic is the deep disturbance that engulfs many Americans who now wonder what it means that voters—albeit less than 25 percent of the electorate, and millions less than the other candidate secured—elected as president, in the fall of 2016, a person who consistently demonstrated what many consider to be the complete lack of a moral compass.

By contrast, however, George Liele was a man with a moral compass. His trustworthiness, which earned him the trust of white church leaders to ordain him to the sacred ministry, his faithfulness to Colonel Kirkland, and his uprightness to find favor with the Jamaican governor, prove this. Liele helped not only Jamaican Baptists, but Jamaica as a whole, to set sail with a compass that led them to salvation, emancipation, education, and development. This is what moral compasses do; and this is the legacy authentic leaders leave.

The transformational authentic handles power appropriately

The proof of the pudding as far as transformational authentics are concerned is how they approach and use power. No diary or journal of George Liele's is available; but from what is available, it would appear that whenever Liele exercised power, it was never with a view to self-aggrandizement or autocracy. Figure 4 illustrates Liele's approach to power. As a Christian minister and student of the Bible, Liele must have known that "there is one who has all the power: Almighty God."[60] Everist and Nessan offer a biblically-positioned definition of transformational leadership: that it "involves

58. Kellerman, *Bad Leadership*, 38–39.

59. Gill, *Theory*, 197–98.

60. Everist and Nessan, *Transforming Leadership*, 54.

clarity about the ministry of the Word, which provides theological vision in all aspects of . . . life. Claiming one's own power and authority does not need to negate the power and authority of others."[61] Hahn identifies four types of authority, including autonomous authority.[62] Of autonomous leaders, she says they know how to share it with stakeholders, instead of grasping it selfishly.[63] It is no surprise that others agree: Greenleaf says, "There is no magic . . . to leading. One simply has . . . to put top priority on building strength in other people."[64] Likewise, Kouzes and Posner, in enlarging on the concept of exemplary leadership practices, affirm that it involves strengthening others.[65] Kellerman however, says something rather curious. She promises to argue that "there's something odd about the idea that somehow leadership can be distinguished from coercion, as if leadership and power were unrelated."[66] In attempting to address the issues of leadership and power, she correctly affirms that they are related; but she employs the word *coercion* which, if used to refer to the way *unethical* leaders use power, is quite correct. We maintain here that in the matter of empowerment, with reference to good (ethical) leaders, it should be considered an unfortunate word, given its overtones of force and duress, and implications of intimidation, arm-twisting, pressure, and manipulation.

61. Ibid., 53.

62. Hahn, *Growing in Authority*, 15–41.

63. Ibid., 18.

64. Spears and Lawrence, *Focus on Leadership*, 251.

65. Kouzes and Posner, *Leadership Challenge*, 248–74.

66. Kellerman, *Bad Leadership*, 4.

Transformational Authentic Leadership — the Empowering Component

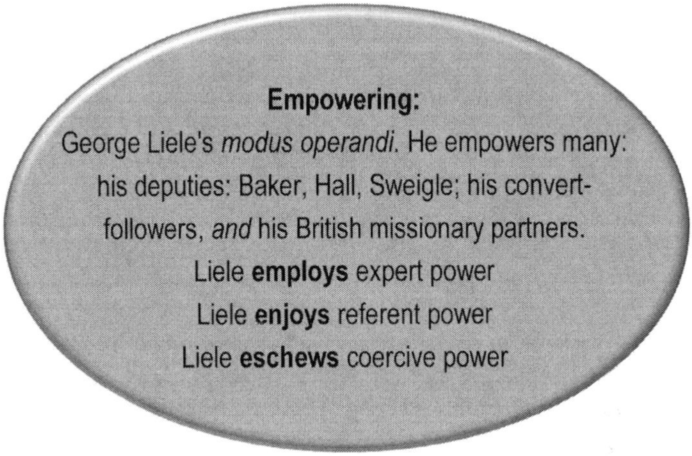

Empowering:

George Liele's *modus operandi.* He empowers many: his deputies: Baker, Hall, Sweigle; his convert-followers, *and* his British missionary partners.

Liele **employs** expert power

Liele **enjoys** referent power

Liele **eschews** coercive power

Figure 4

Although Liele may have endured coercion as a slave, there is no evidence that he exercises it anytime during his ministry and leadership. When Deacon Sweigle tussled (not physically) with him, one might imagine that, were Liele a coercive, autocratic leader, he would not have allowed Sweigle to walk away with many of his (Liele's) members to start another church. This is one of the most enduring testimonies to George Liele as an empowering leader. He could have dug his heels in, laid claim to his congregation, which *he* started and which was *his* domain when Sweigle quarreled with him, challenging his leadership. Yet, Liele did no such thing. He may have read the account where Paul and Barnabas argued, then separated—yet the Word of God spread, anyway;[67] he may have discerned, from his authentic spirit, that allowing Sweigle to walk away was the right thing to do, the best way to expand his own work, the best way of reaching more Jamaican slaves with the gospel, and perhaps, the best way to energize and empower Sweigle himself (who did remarkably well with the churches he planted). There is sufficient information to confidently assert that George Liele was a transformational authentic, who used power for influencing, inducing,

67. Acts 15:36–41.

and enveloping others in a purpose that surpassed his own. He asked for a work, he got a work, and he did it well.

The transformational authentic's intelligence

It is well known that intelligence, with its variety of meanings, has great import for good leadership. George Liele was probably of above-average intelligence. Theories of leadership enable one to go further than simply saying he was smart. Leadership theory holds that there are several intelligences that inform leadership. The ones identified hereafter supremely inform the transformational authentic.

1. *Emotional intelligence.* Daniel Goleman is the guru of emotional intelligence which, as he puts it, is "the ability to manage ourselves and our relationships effectively."[68] Some of the skills into which this intelligence is further subdivided overlap other intelligences below. The extent to which a person may be an effective leader involves the following: first, the extent to which he is aware of his own feelings and self-esteem; second, the extent to which he is equally aware of the dynamics at work in other people with whom he is interacting; third, the extent to which he is able to control himself so as to be predictable, accessible, and amenable to others; and fourth, the extent to which he is able to manage, build, and further healthy relationships with others. For a man to survive slavery to the age of twenty-three, but still, by that very young age, have the respect of slave master, peers, church, community, army colonel, colonial governor, and people—black and white—has to be the sign of a high degree of emotional intelligence. A hothead may neither have survived slavery nor won the respect of so many. Liele's experience as a slave would probably have enhanced his ability to listen to the slaves he now sought to lead, to feel their emotions, to create a church community, to dream of emancipation, and to build an island nation. Perhaps Liele's was a "listening and responding with emotional intelligence that [involved] hearing the people, not just questions or voices."[69]

2. *Social intelligence.* George Liele related well with the mighty and lowly, governor and slave, alike. Liele was the best candidate to model to

68. Goleman, "Leadership That Gets Results," 80.

69. Pearce, *Leading Out Loud,* 134.

blacks—whether slaves or free—values of freedom and salvation. He would have comported himself with great competency, raising equally high ideological goals and high expectations. Liele was a charismatic leader, and he enjoyed the people's referent power, not in any selfish, greedy, or self-serving way, but to re-empower them in return. It is not unreasonable to assume that Liele may have had retentions of *ubuntu* through the conduit of his African ancestry. As mentioned in the previous chapter, ubuntu is deeply invested in community, reciprocity, spirituality, and consensus—the stuff of which social intelligence is made.

3. *Cognitive intelligence.* Reference has already been made to Liele's superior writing skills, evident in his letters. His speech pattern, we could imagine from those letters, might have been commanding, and the content enthralling. The strategy of allowing Sweigle to leave, and intentionally facilitating Moses Baker's appointment to the western end of the island, demonstrates the ability to think, plan, and respond in ways that inspired confidence in others.

4. *Cultural intelligence.* Liele was a culturally agile and versatile human being. He navigated every new culture he entered with aplomb. Not including undocumented moves that are implied and reasonable to imagine that he made, we know he was born in Virginia and moved to Georgia. Although both are considered the American South, those moves were cultural shifts and shocks—as was the move to Jamaica. So too, were the moves from slave to indentured laborer, from indentured to free, from civilian to soldier, from soldier to civilian, from American slave culture to Jamaican slave culture, and from British rule in America to British rule in Jamaica. All this, by one man, in one brief lifetime! Some of these cultural shifts might have been more significant than the others; but that Liele coursed through each with apparent ease demonstrates his cultural intelligence. Liele didn't need to "globalize [his] leadership strategy;"[70] no, he was writing the book on it.

5. *Spiritual intelligence.* For obvious reasons, Liele must have excelled in this intelligence. While morality may not necessarily be grounded in spirituality, for Liele's purposes we might consider the two under the same rubric. In Liele, these two components appear to work in tandem all the time, the one informing the other. Nevertheless, one is

70. Rosen and Digh, "Globally Literate Leaders," 4.

a bit disappointed that, although George[71] affords two paragraphs to the importance of faith in what he calls true north, he does not include one single faith leader among the one hundred twenty-five "authentic leaders" he interviewed for his book.

Transformational Authentic Leadership — George Liele's Intelligences

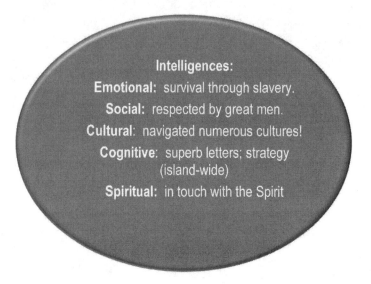

Figure 5

In Figure 5, Liele's various intelligences are summarized. When Figures 2 through 5 are superimposed, they create the whole, single profile of the Transformational Authentic, shown before in figure 1, on page 96.

CHALLENGES TO FRAMING GEORGE LIELE AS A TRANSFORMATIONAL AUTHENTIC

Several questions may arise to challenge George Liele's characterization as a transformational authentic. Among them may be the following: first, if Liele was so authentic, why did he run away from America and leave his baby churches behind? Weren't they the "work" for which he asked? Second, might it not be reasonable to imagine that Liele had some blame to share in the Sweigle incident (perhaps that he was authoritarian), thus

71. George, *True North*.

raising questions about the validity of the claim that he is either authentic or transformational? Third, if Liele was such a team leader, how should one review the Sweigle incident, anyway? Fourth, if Liele was such a transformational authentic, why wasn't he an activist against slavery in his time, like Sam Sharpe and Paul Bogle were in their time (after him), in the Baptist War (the Christmas Day uprising of 1831) and the Morant Bay (1865) incidents, respectively?

Despite the foregoing discourse indirectly answering all of these already, we can offer here some direct answers. Regarding the first, one has to weigh the *outcome* of Liele's move to Jamaica, against the act of leaving America. By any measure, it is undeniable that "a work" developed in Jamaica, and stands today as testimony to his leadership. Second, one has to consider the act of leaving America, not as a cop-out, but as the perseverance of the human spirit, desiring to escape oppression so as to grasp God-given freedom. No one should argue with Liele for seeking freedom. It is one of the driving forces—from time immemorial—for migration. In Liele's case, it is demonstrative of leadership traits such as decisiveness, strength, and intelligence. The fact that he continued "a work" in the new locale is proof of a highly intelligent and visionary leader with an abiding moral compass. It demonstrates his courage, purpose, and authenticity, as well as the strategic thinking necessary to surmount any challenge to lead people to "a promised land". The fact that two of the three churches that Liele started remain alive to this day should say something enduring about their foundation and founder, even if he left them in their infancy.

As far as the question about being authoritarian is concerned, and in the matter of team leadership, it was already suggested that Liele's relationship with Sweigle may be better addressed as a matter of *contingency*, not *transformational*, leadership styles, or may be seen as a plank in his empowerment strategy. Liele empowered Sweigle, to the extent that Sweigle could, albeit in unclear circumstances, feel the autonomy and power to leave, and prove his competence by doing commendable work in another part of Jamaica. This is another measure of Liele's leadership. Liele's release of Sweigle actually accomplished Liele's broad vision, and perhaps in the final analysis, exceeded his or Sweigle's expectations—the very substance of transformational leadership.

Finally, the activism question is a reasonable one. Although this discourse has not delved into Samuel Sharpe or Paul Bogle, both men came of age and to prominence when Liele was an old man, and it is probable that both, being Baptist and slaves, could have been Liele's students. Bogle and Sharpe may have possessed different intelligences than Liele's. This is not to detract from either man's intelligence at all; rather, it is to affirm that Liele's primary calling—his true north—was to preach the gospel, establish congregations, and liberate people spiritually. It is an unassailable argument that, since Bogle and Sharpe were Baptists, the spiritual, religious, biblical, and moral authority on which their activist pursuit of justice and freedom was based, was that which George Liele provided and to which ministry he was called. In that case, he can appropriately be afforded his seat among the activists, having empowered *them* with the some of the intelligences needed for that enterprise.

CONCLUSION

Even though the concepts of self-giving and self-sacrifice have not been named in this profile, it should be clear that these values are at the heart of the transformational authentic. Power-sharing, service, and community-building involve self-giving and sacrifice. The reader and student may dissect this profile back and forth, and use it as the basis for questioning leadership today in any sphere, from church leadership to national leadership. This man transformed a people and a nation. His example can be harvested for developing leadership that transforms congregational, denominational, or even national organizations. If one could find the unmarked grave where he lies, perhaps an apt epitaph might be: "Here Lies the Founder of Baptist Witness in Jamaica; a Transformational Authentic. Here Lies a Competent Leader, Missionary, and Pastor: an African, American and Jamaican Hero, the Honorable George Liele."

Chapter 9

What Churches Need: Managers or Leaders?

CHURCH PEOPLE, CHURCH INSTITUTIONS, and their organizations which do not desire to be led into dysfunction, should prefer principles of leadership to prevail over them, rather than principles of management. As well, they should prefer leaders over managers. Abraham Zaleznik wonders if there is a difference between managers and leaders.[1] A summary of his essay might be in these words: "managers and leaders are very different kinds of people. They differ in motivation, in personal history, and in how they think and act."[2] Managers and leaders differ also in relationships. Northouse adds, "Management was created as a way to reduce chaos in organizations, to make them run more effectively and efficiently."[3] What Northouse does not note is whether the *results* of management's approach are effective or efficient; and if so, at what human cost (bearing in mind, instances and personalities from the business world, such as Wall Street, Enron, Ken Lay, and Jeffrey Skilling). Management focuses on control, competence, the balance of power, order, and quick resolution. Leaders focus on the engines of organizational success: vision, passion, inspiration, and imagination. Managers and leaders have different approaches to the use of power: management nearly invariably seeks to establish who the boss is, or to accumulate and hoard "leadership" advantage because of the need to remain in control. This, of course, limits power-sharing and increases power-distance. Leaders on the other hand approach power as a commodity, *shared* by everyone in

1. Zaleznik, "Managers and Leaders."
2. Ibid., 75.
3. Northouse, *Leadership*, 9.

the community/organization so that everyone may work together toward corporate success.

Management tends to avoid risks, while keeping things ordered and predictable, but leaders do the opposite, not as an end in itself, but in the quest for authenticity, as well as in the pursuit of goals that match either theirs or their communities' values and vision. This approach removes power from the status quo—and in the best scenarios, even eliminates the status quo. Managers, on the other hand, seem to *need* the status quo; that is, if they do not seek to be the status quo themselves.

Because managers ordinarily are answerable and accountable to bosses (the very notion of management) in the form of boards or chief executive officers (CEOs), their world can often involve concern about their own skin. Leaders, on the other hand, by virtue of the latitude they possess in charting the course of the entity or organization, are accountable only to the people they lead. If the leader engages the members of the organization in the formation of its values, vision, and mission, and if these followers own the initiative, then the leader escapes the kind of pressure that more likely attends the manager, whose followers, ordinarily, do not share in formulating the organization's vision and mission. Indeed, in the worst case scenario, the manager may not even share the organization's vision or mission; that may be all set by a board, to the exclusion of others, including the manager! Boards and the managers they employ tend to care about the bottom line, and the tasks and mission; leaders care about the needs of followers and, where they are ethically sound, seldom give attention to their own skin. Managers tend to adopt impersonal, if not passive, attitudes toward goals, while leaders question, rethink, and recalibrate goals. This, because the manager enters someone else's goals (the Board or the CEO); whereas, the leader pursues goals that have been shaped by herself and her team—the member-workers or followers. Because of this, in the worst manager-run organization, fewer followers might have a clue about the reason for the goals they and their manager must meet; while, in the *true* leader-run organization, everyone is likely to know, provided the leader has employed the skills, strategies, and techniques which effective leaders do, for creating and communicating vision and purpose.

Zaleznik notes that "a managerial culture emphasizes rationality and control . . . a manager is a problem solver."[4] But the leadership student knows that leadership (especially transformational leadership) is about

4. Zaleznik, "Managers and Leaders," 75.

adaptive—not technical—change; it is about team energy, not leader dictates; it is about the power of all to understand, imagine, address, and create (and solve problems along the way, too), not the power of one individual to solve. The manager is burdened with the weight of addressing the life of the organization and its sustenance (more out of being between the devil of the demands of upper management and the deep blue sea of saving his own skin!), while the leader harnesses all the followers' energies and imaginations joyfully enlisting them in that enterprise, free from the dictates of any extraneous entity.

We should not draw the line between leaders and managers too thickly, though. Says Zaleznik: "It takes neither genius nor heroism to be a manager, but rather persistence, tough-mindedness, hard work, intelligence, analytical ability, and perhaps most important, tolerance and goodwill."[5] All of these descriptors are quite apt for leaders too; one certainly does not imagine that Zaleznik was suggesting they do not. He suggests that managers emerge through "socialization, which prepares the individual to guide institutions and to maintain the existing balance of social relations," while leaders "develop through personal mastery, which impels an individual to struggle for psychological and social change."[6] We maintain that effective leaders develop through *both,* as well as do some managers.

Compared to leaders, managers may have some limitations, a few of which Zaleznik recognizes. One of them relates to growth. He asks, "is it true that no matter how competent managers are, their leadership stagnates because of their limitations in visualizing purposes and generating value in work?"[7] The answer, of course, is quite often yes. One of the major differences between managers and leaders is growth, which flows from imagination, creativity, and breadth and depth of perspective. Of the two, managers suffer the greater risk of stagnation. They may be hamstrung by dictates rather than possibilities, and constancy, rather than change. They may find that they have no latitude, initiative, or autonomy to create or rethink goals. They may find it difficult to differentiate between themselves and their tasks, thus valuing themselves by the metric of their tasks and success. They may come to find their tasks more important than the people they manage; indeed, they understand that it is *people* they manage—not *things!* They may find themselves beholden to three bottom lines: their bosses' approval, the

5. Ibid.
6. Ibid., 79.
7. Ibid., 75.

company's financial well-being, and of course, saving their own position. Bad leaders may succumb to one of more of these same dictates. But the leadership environment—in contrast to the managerial—offers more scope for authentic purpose, vision, values, and an relationship between the organization's members and leaders.

It is precisely because of this that ironically, even though it is said that managers consider themselves called to be fixers, their so-called fixes are often with a view to maintaining the status quo. Compared to leaders, they may find insufficient opportunity for decisiveness and the freshness and inspiration that emanate from engaging in developing vision, purpose, ideals, or goals. Their "fixes" may also tend to be safer than riskier. When problems arise, especially due to upper management or lower management's fault, scapegoating is highly likely, and tactics, including subterfuge, deception, prevarication, and more, are deployed. Things might be quite different in the leader-led environment. There, the members and leaders would have shared in the situation that produced the problem; they would probably have committed themselves to learning from any problems that arose. In that case, the scapegoating tactics to which a manager might resort would not be necessary. This is precisely the approach that Toyota, referred to earlier, took toward problems on their assembly lines, thereby empowering everyone to share in decision-making, and revolutionizing the concept of management. Managers may try to fix contradictions (or circumvent them); leaders tend to view contradictions as cues for reflection, rethinking, evaluating, reframing, and re-visioning, the result of which could be new energy for the organization and its human relationships. Leaders use contradictions as tools that can *lead* to transformation, and to solutions that exceed the desires or dreams of only one person.

We repeat, though, that we are offering a classical, if not pedantic, description of the difference between managers and leaders. It is worth repeating that the line between them should not be thought of as being too wide. Finally, in a discourse that uses, curiously, a term Christians may interpret howsoever they wish, Zaleznik refers to personalities that are once-born, versus those that are twice-born.[8] Once-born leaders "are those for whom adjustments to life have been straightforward and whose lives have been more or less a peaceful flow since birth. Twice-borns, on the other hand, have not had an easy time of it. Their lives are marked by a continual struggle to

8. Ibid., 79. It is Christian jargon, because Zaleznik is referring to William James in "The Varieties of Religious Experience."

attain some sense of order. Unlike once-borns, they cannot take things for granted."[9] This is exactly the idea of authenticity that was at work in preparing George Liele for leadership. Zaleznik never states that managers are once borns; but he does clearly say, "Leaders tend to be twice-born personalities, people who feel separate from their environment. They may work in organizations, but they never belong to them. Their sense of who they are does not depend on memberships, work roles, or other social indicators of identity."[10] This idea of being in the organization but not belonging to it is Gunderson's thesis, where he argues that a special kind of persons whom he calls *boundary leaders* lead on the edge of the organization, always ready to go beyond where the organization is, currently.[11]

CONGREGATIONAL AND DENOMINATIONAL ORGANIZATIONS NEED LEADERS, NOT MANAGERS.

Managers manage things, and leaders lead people. The church's people are not things.

Do churches, congregations, denominations, and their organizations need managers or leaders? There is perhaps room for managers in every organization. But the fact is this: managers should manage things, and leaders should lead people. When managers try to manage people, they extract from them less than might be desired. It does not stop there; they also extract less from the *relationship*, likely to be difficult between manager and people. This would be the diametric opposite to what is envisaged in and expected of leadership, especially of the transformational kind. Further, when organizations are designed on any basis or structure that results in managing people, that organization is certain to become unhealthy, unhappy, and less productive than it otherwise could be. It is particularly lamentable when that organization is a congregation, or denomination, or religious entity.

Some pastors know very well, the bane of management reposing itself (or being *imposed*) where, instead, leadership should prevail. Some pastors have worked in an environment where the deacons, or elders, or board, or

9. Ibid.
10. Ibid.
11. Gunderson, *Boundary Leaders*.

council, or presbyters, or other lay leaders, consider themselves the pastors' employers, supervisors, bosses, and managers. Such pastors know the bane of being managed, rather than being allowed to lead. Zaleznik observes that managers "typically become very anxious in the relative disorder that leaders seem to generate."[12] Where, in churches, pastors and/or congregations are considered to be subject to the deacons or other lay leaders' management, the organization becomes not only confusing and potentially contentious, but also ineffective and dysfunctional. While Zaleznik observes that "human relations in leader-dominated structures often appear turbulent, intense, and at times even disorganized,"[13] he could have made the comment about manager-led organizations too.

Managers are "once-born"; leaders are "twice-born." The church's people are "twice-born".

It is intriguing that leaders are described as twice-born; for this raises an idiom with which the church, especially of the evangelical strain, is familiar: *born again*. Born-again leaders—people who are birthed spiritually, not just naturally[14]—are required no more desperately anywhere, than in congregational and denominational life. Both the idea of spiritual rebirth, and the idea of crucial life-changing experiences that recreate or rebirth a person, are necessary for good leadership in church institutions. Further, the idea of being separate from an environment—within it but not belonging to it—relates closely to another biblical truth. As Jesus was facing the end of his earthly ministry, he prayed for the new leaders he had just spent three years forming, that though they were in the world, they were not of it.[15] Indeed, a major key to Jesus's success in the world was that he too, was not of the world, though in it.[16] And now, apostolic leadership was going to require that these men knew what it meant to be in the world, but not of it. Ultimately, in our time, effective congregational and denominational leaders—whether ordained or not—would be served well to wrestle also, with what it means to be in the organization, but not of it. Managers, however, by the very nature of what they are called to be and expected to do, are tethered to their organizations, and

12. Zaleznik, "Managers and Leaders," 75.
13. Ibid., 79.
14. John 3:3–8.
15. John 17:14–16.
16. Ibid.

committed to the limitations thereof. In this prayer of Jesus, one of his reasons for leading emerges: it is to develop leaders. We recall Avolio and Bass's position that "true transformational leaders . . . convert their followers into leaders."[17] Jesus did not only *convert* his followers into leaders; he *rebirthed* them into leaders; and we know that, organically, reproduction is always only after its own kind. Consequently we can conclude that, ordinarily, leaders produce leaders and managers produce managers.

Leaders are more risk-averse than managers. The church's people are to be risk-takers.

Because leaders are free to engage followers to chart their own course together as an organization, leaders are likely to take greater risks than managers, who are given marching orders by somebody above, and often with no reference to the people under the manager's supervision. Church institutions and organizations are, as Christ-followers, risk-prone; this, no matter how risk-averse they seek to be! In the exercise of obedience to Jesus and following his mission, Christ-followers are exposed to dangers. The disciples, in obedience to Jesus's instruction to set sail for the other side of the Sea of Galilee, immediately discovered that there was considerable risk to be encountered in following Jesus.[18]

The church and its brave leaders and members are always tested with the dilemma of when to remain tethered to the traditional and popular, and when to launch out to new and unfamiliar paradigms, risking ridicule and even rejection. Martin Luther King Jr. was the latter, while a group of clergy to whom he wrote was the former. Jailed for the risky and unusual business of leading the fight for civil rights, he penned his famous letter from a Birmingham jail, in which he felt constrained for the first time to defend his departure from what the church ordinarily expected of its clergy. In it, King lamented:

> I have been disappointed with the church. I do not say this as one of those negative critics who can always find something wrong with the church. I say this as a minister of the gospel, who loves the church; who was nurtured in its bosom; who has been sustained by its spiritual blessings and who will remain true to it as long as the cord of life shall lengthen . . . I felt that . . . ministers,

17. Avolio and Bass, *Developing Potential*, 1.

18. Mark 4:35–41.

priests and rabbis . . . would be among our strongest allies. Instead, some have been outright opponents . . . too many others have been more cautious than courageous and have remained silent behind the anesthetizing security of stained glass windows.[19]

What King's leadership wrought is well-documented in history; and whenever the church chooses to remain shackled to conservative risk-aversion, it always passes up opportunities for "turning the world upside down"[20] in desperately desired and necessary ways.

Management concerns programs more than people. The church—as people—needs leaders.

Because management is, properly, more about overseeing programs, managing resources, and less about the development of people, one of the more prevalent complaints about people who are under the supervision of managers, or under the leadership of bad leaders, is that they feel stifled or otherwise prevented to grow. Initiative is retarded, and creativity takes a hit. That the church and its members are described as a body and individual members of it, respectively,[21] means that first, like an organism, the church and its members are meant to grow. Each member of this body is to be free to exercise its unique capabilities and capacities. That Jesus would include one such as Judas in his bunch of disciples speaks in some way to the initiative Jesus allows Judas to develop, and the latitude to learn a new way despite the way he eventually chose. Given that broad truth, is it at all possible that when Jesus says to Judas, "What you are going to do, do quickly,"[22] that this is not necessarily, "Go finish what you started" but, instead, "My friend, you have an opportunity still, at this point, to choose"? One could not expect Jesus to incite or hasten someone to evil, so the question is valid. Either way, Jesus left the decision up to Judas, even though the wrong decision would be made. Even though risk is taken when latitude, autonomy, and initiative are given to others, and even though the liability can be distressing if things go wrong, the best environment in which growth is encouraged and in which leadership is cultivated is where people

19. King, "Letter," paragraphs 26–27.
20. Acts 17:6 (KJV).
21. See 1 Cor 12.
22. John 13:27.

are given the space to grow. That includes the freedom to make mistakes, while in the process of exercising initiative and creativity. When initiative and creativity yield happy results, the payback can be enormous.

When congregational and denominational organizations choose to install leaders within the various parts of these entities, there is a reason less management would be required. If management is more appropriate for deployment over things and programs so as to ensure that the work objectives are met, then we maintain that in the church and its organizations, leadership is better. As a living organism—such as a body—is healthy when each organ and part is working well, so too the church is declared to be healthy, effective, efficient, mature, wholesome, and successful, when "each parts does its work."[23] How does the church arrive at this? It does, because it is adequately equipped with leaders[24] who understand that their role is not to manage people, but instead, to develop, empower and "equip"[25] them. When church and denominational institutions deploy leaders, not managers, in the right locations, and when such leaders understand themselves as leaders, not managers, the result is that the work—which is what requires management, not the people—shall be adequately taken care of, as each person does their work.

23. Eph 4:16.
24. Ibid., verse 11.
25. Ibid., verse 12.

PART III

Our Churches Can Do Better—And They Should

Continuous improvement is better than delayed perfection.
—*Mark Twain*

Curious that we spend more time congratulating people who have succeeded than encouraging people who have not.
—*Neil deGrasse Tyson*

One of the great mistakes is to judge policies and programs by their intentions rather than their results.
—*Milton Friedman*

You never know what is enough unless you know what is more than enough.
—*William Blake*

If you are building a culture where honest expectations are communicated and peer accountability is the norm, then the group will address poor performance and attitudes.
—*Henry Cloud*

Chapter 10

Enhancing and Evaluating Church People's Ministry Performance

CHURCH PEOPLE, CHURCH INSTITUTIONS, and their organizations which do not desire to be led into dysfunction, should provide a robust performance management system as well as a fair and encouraging evaluation process for their leaders and members. Before an organization could, with fairness and with some modicum of relevance or even accuracy, do an evaluation of its people or of its ministries, that organization should understand something about performance management. If a person's performance were to be evaluated in the absence of a system that pursues the enhancement of *both* that person's ministry/job performance, and the environment in which that person is expected to perform, then the evaluation is likely to produce skewed results. These results often disfavor the individual more than they do the organization. In many cases, it is the latter that should be scrutinized; in all cases, it should be both.

Garth Walton enjoyed, but sometimes endured, his four-decade career in pastoral and congregational ministry, in several different assignments. During that time, Walton also served his denomination in several functions. While his denominational positions were honorary and without remuneration, his pastoral assignments were paid positions. As pastor, Walton was generally considered to be "in charge"; but at the same time he was also *employee* of the very people over whom he was in charge. None of Walton's churches had a human resource (HR) department or officer. Walton knows what *forced termination* means: it is a term that applies to pastors who are summarily dismissed, or made to resign involuntarily, or otherwise deliberately and intentionally frustrated toward voluntary resignation from their pastoral assignments. Walton is familiar with all three avenues of forced termination. As he looks back on his experiences, he is certain that each time he was dismissed or forced toward resignation, it was done improperly, according to all the best known HR processes and practices. In at least one of those cases, he was also dismissed illegally, and would have won that case in a court of law had he had the resources, or stamina, or will, to pursue it there.

There are many issues underlying Walton's experiences. One has to do with spiritual maturity; another, with many of the leadership issues explored so far. There are many pastors, though, who (unlike Walton) have never been fired or who have never felt deliberately frustrated toward a resignation, but who nevertheless have either resigned in frustration, or plod along in their pastorates under a pall of frustration. In Walton and these pastors' cases, a chief underlying cause is the paucity of HR practices and HR systems, including poor—or absent—performance management systems. One of the most distinct pieces of evidence that churches do not consider themselves governed or governable by many of the healthy and wise practices that govern other organizations, is the absence of proper HR procedures, even where, in those *very* congregations, are persons who *do* report to work, Monday through Friday, week after week, in HR departments in corporate America!

The average congregation's mission and business goals are, in a word, *growth*. In the average congregation, there are five areas in which growth may be desired: (1) personal growth, (2) spiritual growth, (3) missional growth, (4) numerical growth, and (5) financial growth. It is difficult, though not impossible, to both define and measure the first three of these five areas. It is not uncommon to find that too many congregations, therefore, end up *not* defining, either properly or at all, what personal, spiritual, or missional growth are, what they look like, or what their parameters might be. Because these three areas present this kind of definition and measurement challenge, congregational and denominational organizations and their people often focus inordinately and disproportionately on the other two areas of growth (numerical and financial). They do this even though a case can be made to show that, while important, they might be considered to be of less import than the others.

Walton, as he reflects on his forty-one years of ministry, muses that, as far as performance evaluations and performance strategies are concerned, the congregations he has served appear to have the general notion that the sum total of their performance strategy is to preach the gospel, have attractive or "exciting" worship services, and some kind of "exciting" children and youth program. The success of these would be measured, of course, by attendance, membership, and financial growth.

Until Walton learned about performance management late in his career, results in congregational and denominational life had to do with expectations and hope, and nearly nothing to do with management and systems. People expected that everyone would do their work, the Lord would bless it, and then they would see results; but nothing was managed, systematized, or choreographed toward performance or results. Walton affirms that, what appears to be the sum total of his, and many of his colleagues' congregational and denominational organizations' performance strategy, are congregational meetings, council or board meetings, deacons and elders' meetings, and the occasional committee meetings; in other words, meetings, meetings, and meetings. While there is nothing wrong with meetings *per se,* Walton's account of the content of these meetings demonstrates the absence of performance strategy and performance management, and mirror the experiences with which many pastors and parishioners would identify:

- *Congregational meetings* (ranging from once a year to once a quarter) offer the congregation (often much less than half the membership) opportunities to discuss general matters. Sometimes it is even less than that—it may be to hear reports from committees and leaders. Again, it sometimes may be even less than *that*: to vote on proposals, the development of which they may have had nothing to do. This is hardly performance management.

- *Council or board meetings* (usually monthly) gather the ordained and non-ordained leaders for more concentrated oversight over the church's work, for reporting on what has been (or not) done; and for discussion on what remains to be done. This, too, is hardly performance management.

- *Deacons and elders' meetings* (mostly with a monthly frequency) in some contexts, address the personal and spiritual concerns of the congregation; and in other contexts concern themselves with administrative, property, and financial matters. While this might be financial and property management, it is hardly performance management.

Congregations that employ and remunerate their own pastors (versus the ones where a number of congregations pool their resources, and a bishop or other administrator appoints the pastor and/or the single denominational organization pays its pastors) find themselves in the potentially complicated situation where a pastor is both employee and chief leader. At the same time, the parishioners are also both employers and (volunteer) employees, as well as financially contributing stakeholders! This situation could be a challenge for the health of the church organization and the relationships within. In such congregations—perhaps more than in any other kind of enterprise, or job, or employment arrangement— a performance management system may be crucial, if not indispensable. If such churches do not implement some such system, the pastor's job, as well as pastoral and congregational relationships, could almost certainly be fraught with significant tensions, conflicts, and challenge.

The congregations with which Walton and the average parishioner and pastor are familiar, appear to consider their congregational meetings, council or board meetings, deacons and elders meetings, and other committee or sectional meetings adequate for regulating their congregations' performance. Walton certainly never gave it a thought before he awakened to the concept of performance management and evaluation. But the reality is that while these meetings are important for the congregations' meaningful function, they might be considered a kind of infrastructure that suffers from the lack of a superstructure. By superstructure, we are referring to the measures that are embraced by and govern the people, the agenda, and the objectives of the many congregational and organizational meetings. This superstructure is to ensure that the best performance is secured from all the persons who are expected to do what these meetings imply and require that they do.

This is where church organizations should seek to become adequate, knowledgeable, and concerned about putting a proper HR superstructure upon their organized meetings, which we call the infrastructure. When they do this, it would result in the following: (1) they will pursue clearly defined goals that are measurable, time-sensitive, and attainable; (2) they would pursue specific tasks assigned to specific people; (3) they shall pursue enforceable accountability measures of all their leaders, people, and ministry performers; (4) they shall pursue measures that can correct or replace, if needed, persons who breach the congregation's values, especially if with impunity; (5) they shall pursue formal performance review processes of their pastoral and other ministry leaders, committee leaders, and other key functionaries in the congregation. However, when church organizations fail to do this, they pursue, instead, a recipe for dysfunction—a dysfunction that goes on undetected, in congregations; since, after all, church people tend to declare nonchalantly, "we trust in the Holy Spirit, not in men." Walton recalls that in one of the congregations from which he resigned, nearly 4 percent of the members were persons who occupied, or have occupied, *senior* HR positions in companies in secular life. He recalls how unconcerned they were about his being forced to resign without due process, which could have been successfully prosecuted had it been litigated in secular America.

When church organizations fail to put HR superstructures in place, their staff—especially pastoral or denominational leaders—may be improperly, inadequately, unfairly, or incorrectly assessed, and subsequently unfairly dismissed or terminated. Indeed, while clergy leaders are the ones likely to be forced out or viewed as the congregation's stumbling block to health, poorly performing lay leaders (especially those who feel they are there to "manage" the clergy) remain in place, unfettered. In Walton's experience, lay leaders are never assessed and criticized as much as the pastor. Walton certainly feels that in such cases, having no assessment might in fact have been less harmful to the churches (and certainly himself!) than the deficient and injurious ones that were used.

BUILDING A MINISTRY PERFORMANCE ENHANCEMENT AND MANAGEMENT SUPERSTRUCTURE

If the average congregation resembles any of Walton's, there is hope, despite the challenges. Congregational and denominational meetings actually represent tremendous opportunity, if the content were to be reexamined, refreshed, and redesigned to scratch where the organizations itch. These meetings should painstakingly seek to address the congregations' organizational, operational, and developmental issues, to listen to the *real* concerns of the members, and to help them reimagine ministry, and the pursuit of life together as a people of faith. In all of this, the guiding questions should include: How can we do this better? How can this be life-giving to all who are involved? How shall we know that it is time to move on to something else? How could this bring joy to others and a sense of fulfillment to us?

As church organizations build a ministry performance enhancement superstructure, there are several planks that must be installed, including balance, deeply embedded life interests, collective intelligence, motivation and rewards, communication, and setting expectations.

Ministry performance enhancement superstructure, plank 1: balance

Congregations' growth goals (personal, spiritual, missional, numerical, and financial growth) present the perfect framework and opportunity for congregations and church organizations to begin to design balanced score cards for their leaders, members, employees, workers, and volunteers. "The balanced scorecard is a method of evaluation that uses four specific, balanced perspectives to measure performance: financial, customer, internal business processes, and learning and growth."[1] Of course, in their creativity, church organizations can reframe or reinterpret those four areas into the ministry and growth-specific areas that apply to them. For example, "customer" and "business" are words that may be foreign to the church on the surface; but when reframed and reviewed in a church context, can produce a deeper appreciation for what church organizations are meant to do in becoming efficient and effective. Congregations' five basic growth goals (personal, spiritual, missional, numerical, and financial) may fit like hand and glove with Smith and Mazin's four perspectives:

- Financial growth pairs with *financial*;

- Missional (outreach and service to the community) pairs with *customer*;

- Personal and spiritual growth (worship, fellowship, vision, maintenance of unity and a healthy, joyful and life-giving church environment) pairs with *internal business processes*; and

- All forms of congregational growth pair with *learning and growth*.

But balance goes beyond a balanced score card employing these four basic and broad areas of evaluation; balance also addresses balanced performance expectations. It is neither balanced nor fair for a pastor's job description to be drafted, but no congregational behavioral covenant, code, or expectations established. Sheryl Healy, throughout her five-year tenure at Bethel Church, would regularly urge the leaders about the need for a behavioral covenant that would govern how members and leaders should behave in times of trouble and organizational crisis or stress. She would always urge that the best time to develop this covenant was when the congregation was enjoying peace and good health. Bethel's key leaders would always respond that a behavioral covenant was a good idea, but not urgent. It is that same behavioral covenant that might have bound members to act differently, after

---

1. Smith and Mazin, *HR Answer*, 53.

Healy was forced to resign, following a leaders' meeting where she was blind-sided and ambushed. (Healy was never evaluated nor offered any substantial reason for this.) After submitting her resignation, Healy and her family were practically excommunicated—the church's leaders never acknowledged or otherwise responded to her gracious resignation letter; the congregation never thanked her for her service or said goodbye; and apart from four exceptions, no members called, wrote, visited, or commiserated. Several weeks after Healy resigned, one of the church's families walked past her at a convenience store, as though she were a piece of furniture. The crime that Healy committed was not child abuse; neither was it pornography nor fiduciary irresponsibility, or pastoral ineptitude. Healy's termination by six lay leaders stemmed from her audacity in selecting the hymn of her choice for a worship service—an act that annoyed the worship leader!

Congregations present significant potential as the best places for what is known as three-hundred-sixty-degree evaluation. This is feedback which, ordinarily, an employee receives anonymously from other employees, whom the employee supervises, to whom the employee reports, and with whom the employee shares rank parity. In its more sophisticated iteration, the feedback is collected online. Both the target and their evaluators complete a series of questions aimed at evaluating the target's performance, aptitude, attitudes, and a range of other metrics, in the pursuit of a balanced evaluation. The online assessment agency collates the information and issues the results. In congregations, this might be a healthy exercise whether the culture is hierarchical or not; especially if it is a hierarchical culture, and especially if all the congregation's leaders and key people were to submit to it, the benefits to the leaders' performance in particular, and the organizations' in general, can be enormous.

Ministry performance enhancement superstructure, plank 2: deeply embedded life interests

"Deeply embedded life interests are long-held, emotionally driven lifelong passions, intricately entwined with personality and thus born of an indeterminate mix of nature and nurture."[2] If an organization's leaders desire an individual to perform and function effectively and optimally in any given role, they would do well to discover what that person's embedded life interests (ELIs) are. "Deeply embedded life interests do not determine what

2. Butler and Waldroop, "Job Sculpting," 145–46.

people are good at—they drive what kinds of activities make them happy. At work, that happiness often translates into commitment. It keeps people engaged, and it keeps them from quitting."[3] Simply put, when ELIs are discovered, they enable people to follow their passions, tailoring them to the tasks before them. Butler and Waldroop identify eight ELIs which they call "the big eight":[4]

1. Application of technology

2. Quantitative analysis

3. Theory development and conceptual thinking

4. Creative production

5. Counseling and mentoring

6. Managing people and relationships

7. Enterprise control

8. Influence through language and ideas.[5]

Just as—with the spiritual gifts that Paul lists in 1 Cor 12—a person may have one or more gifts but never all of them, so it is with the ELIs: a person may have more than one, but never all of them. The various combinations present interesting opportunities and competencies.

Even though no individual may have all of these ELIs, congregations need to be careful that they do not *expect* their pastors to be proficient in or able to function with all of them any or all of the time (and certainly, not all at the same time). The operative words are *all of the time*; for pastors can possibly function in each interest from time to time, even if it may not be deeply embedded in him or her. For example, as preacher and teacher, the pastor may function with *influence through language and ideas*, and with *technological applications*: computers, PowerPoint, and video clips. As shepherd, the pastor may function with *counseling and mentoring people, and relationship management*. As planner, and leading the flock into the future, pastors may engage in *theory development and conceptual thinking*, as well as with *creative production*, which they had better have applied to their sermons too! Finally, as church manager and administrator, they may function with *enterprise control* and *quantitative analysis*. In the same way

3. Ibid., 146.

4. Ibid., 148.

5. Ibid., 148–52.

that Paul encourages Timothy to "do the work of an evangelist,"[6] while he may or may not have had that particular spiritual gift, pastors may need to engage in work from time to time in which their primary interests do not lie. For best performance though, congregational and church organizations might take an inventory of their leaders and members' ELIs and determine what functions in their organizations are best served by these ELIs. When people are encouraged to pursue functions that are supported by their ELIs, they can be expected to perform better. Additionally, these organizations may better arrange personnel in ways that ensure that one person's interests and functions are complemented by another's—just as with the distribution and deployment of spiritual gifts.

Butler and Waldroop's "big eight" are not exhaustive, just (as most theologians conclude) the lists of spiritual gifts in 1 Cor 12, Eph 4, Rom 12, and 1 Pet 4 are not exhaustive. It can be said, for example, that physical prowess is an embedded life interest, which is what leads people to be sportsmen and women, Olympic athletes and medalists. Altruism may be an ELI; it is the deep liking for people and their causes, and a driving interest in helping them. A church organization's intentional aligning of their personnel's jobs, tasks, and ministry functions with the personnel's passions or deeply embedded life interests augurs well for shaping the personnel toward high performance and is a step toward excellence in managing performance.

Ministry performance enhancement superstructure, plank 3: collective intelligence

The definition of collective intelligence is as predictable as it is logical. It is the gathering of intelligence from all the members of a group as they share, collaborate, discuss, exchange, cross-pollenate, and sharpen ideas and information with each other. It should be clear to see how, when this type of intelligence is promoted, the church organization may embrace corporate responsibility and accountability, and enjoy an efficiency garnered from the entire community. Collective intelligence wards off territorial behaviors; it tempers superiority behaviors and the marginalization of member-stakeholders who some might consider less resourceful, or intelligent, or useful, or even worthy of being heard.[7] All this while reducing the chance

6. 2 Tim 4:5.

7. These attitudes are not unique only to secular organizations; they are quite alive

of autocracy and unilateralism. It communicates welcome and belonging to the participants, and contributes to team building along the way. All of this then redounds to the better performance of the organization's leaders and people.

There are several steps a church organization may take if it wishes to create a culture that encourages and engenders collective intelligence:

1. *Build strong and healthy relationships,* in which high value is placed on mutual courtesy, respect, and regular celebration of individuals' gifts and skills, at every stratum of the organization.

2. Install *clear guidelines, standards, and indicators* that might accomplish these strong relationships.

3. Pursue *intentional team-building,* in which the power of the team is constantly emphasized over the power of individuals, or at least held in balance with it.

4. *Share information:* each organization would need to determine, in keeping with their unique circumstances, culture, context, and objectives, the parameters and criteria that govern what should be shared and shareable. One of the ways that power can be abused, and one of the ways in which toxic leadership is made manifest, is by manipulating information,[8] or being manipulative on a whole. Manipulating information (and people) is one of the easiest ways to retain intelligence and power in one individual, so as to toxically increase prestige, while starving colleagues and the organization of intelligence that would redound to not only the success of the organization, but to the reduction of stress in the organization or workplace.

One of the problems that Dahlia Crandall[9] encountered with Eric James was precisely this manipulation of information. As general secretary of the Valencia Fellowship of churches, James was the recipient of all correspondence from other states, other denominations, and the international body of the denomination. James revealed—even to president Crandall, as well as the executive committee she chaired—what he wanted to, and concealed what he wanted to, all in bad faith, bad

and manifestly evident in church organizations. The "Kingdom" church —Terry Fellowes, pastor—is one such exhibit; and there are more, not only congregationally, but also denominationally.

8. See Bass and Steidlmeier, "Ethics", 181–217.

9. See chapter 5.

stewardship, and bad leadership. The result was anything but collective intelligence. Indeed, in the fateful meeting that Crandall called, but did not chair, and from which James walked out in a huff, Ramsey (the vice-chair) made a most revealing and groveling statement to James, when he threatened to walk out: "You are the repository of knowledge in this Fellowship! Please don't leave." The absence of collective intelligence in churches and church organizations is nothing short of a tragedy.

5. Another step toward creating a culture that celebrates and engenders collective intelligence is *continuing education*. There are not a few churches today where the prevailing thought about Christian education is that it is for children and not adults. Many churches offer a midweek Bible study or continuing education opportunity for the membership, where the most notably absent participants are the churches' non-or-dained (or lay) leaders, including deacons and Sunday school teachers. Churches may derive great value from special seminars or workshops either held in-house or in retreat format off-campus. The old adage is that the family that prays together stays together; the benefits, however, from studying and learning together are immeasurable, especially when intentionally understood by all as aimed at improving performance among all of the organization's people.

6. *Experiment with performance review structures.* The church should seek to engage many of its members and leaders in the performance evaluation of as many others in the congregation, denomination or organization. This would provide greater opportunity for not only sharing information, but also for gathering information and intelligence. The more church organizations understand that performance evaluation is more about the entire organization, even when focusing on certain of its leaders and people, the more people might observe, research, study, and discuss the organizations in terms broader than just their individual leaders.

7. In the beginning of this section, we observed that collective intelligence implies collective responsibility. A seventh and final step we offer for building a culture of collective intelligence is *education about collective intelligence itself*; for collective intelligence also means collective responsibility. In political life, especially for presidential or prime ministerial cabinets that follow the Westminster model, collective responsibility means that whatever the cabinet agrees, each

individual minister or secretary must hold, adopt, and agree, or else resign. However, in organizations where collective intelligence is pursued and upheld, collective responsibility should mean that no single person should ever be scapegoated anymore for anything that goes wrong in the organization. It does not mean that he or she gets to hide behind a crowd for infractions or decisions which they might have made unilaterally or outside of the ambit of the collective intelligence; but it does create a safety net for all of the associates, partners, participants, and leaders, at any stratum of the congregation, denomination, or organization, to share their ideas without fear of recrimination. Churches—much like sporting institutions which fire their coaches—have a penchant for blaming the pastor when the church becomes something less than what people think it should be. This is often an appropriate move, but it may also be scapegoating, where the institution is unwilling to take responsibility for itself.

Ministry performance enhancement superstructure, plank 4: motivation and rewards

It is a truth from time immemorial that human beings are motivated by rewards. In secular life and organizations, money is regularly included among the primary motivators and rewards for good performance. Scholars explore two major sources of motivation—intrinsic and extrinsic.[10] One of them says, "Intrinsic motivation—being motivated by challenge and enjoyment—is essential to creativity. But extrinsic motivation—being motivated by recognition and money—doesn't necessarily hurt."[11] An example of intrinsic motivation is "artists . . . [who] tended to be motivated more by challenge, but . . . also . . . by recognition."[12] Another responds: "Productivity and performance improve the most when work is reorganized so that employees have the training, opportunity, and authority to participate effectively in decision-making; when they have assurances that they will not be punished for expressing unpopular ideas."[13] Still another concludes that

10. Stewart et al., "Rethinking Rewards," 3–11.
11. Ibid., 7.
12. Ibid.
13. Ibid., 5.

managers need "to stop manipulating employees with rewards and punishments and . . . stop pushing money into their faces."[14]

When all of these are taken together, no reasonable argument can be made against keeping rewards on the table, unless reasonable doubt prevails that rewards do not work. It is not just a matter of rewards that are offered; the kind of reward as well as its aim are equally important. In the church, money may be far less of a motivator or reward than in corporate and secular institutions. But even in the latter, there remains much evidence that it is not money, primarily, that motivates workers. There are many other less expensive, and more productive and extrinsic measures that employers can use, which appeal to workers' intrinsic values (and source of motivation) so as to make both job satisfaction and organizational output increase.

For congregations and denominational organizations, intrinsic motivation emanates from the satisfaction that it is God who calls, equips, energizes, and walks alongside workers. They understand that God is guiding them, and this is a source of motivation. Additionally, the joy of doing God's work, especially when lives are evidently blessed and benefitted (though some may label this as extrinsic motivation), truly energizes the church worker. As far as extrinsic motivation is concerned, church organizations employ various forms of it to enhance performance: pastor appreciation events, birthday and anniversary events of members, special mention in public worship of persons who serve in special ways, or serve well, or serve long, and the identification of new leaders, giving them responsibility. After all, "employees are motivated by . . . assuming increased levels of responsibility."[15] In some congregations, some parishioners hide from positions of responsibility; in others, they relish them. But people need responsibility, achievement, affiliation, and the exercise of power as propellants and motivators; they need *content*—which is why this is understood as the *content theory* of motivation.[16]

In congregations, the need for affiliation and power is strong; congregational dysfunction is due mostly to power plays and power struggles (arising from faulty affiliation or disaffiliation), or some misuse or abuse of power. When congregations and Christian organizations get relationships right, with copious volumes of affiliation, understanding, mutual respect, cooperation, thoughtful distribution of power, sharing of power, and

14. Ibid., 11.

15. Pynes, *Human Resource Management*, 216.

16. Ibid., 220.

discover conscientious ways of recognizing the value in each member and participant and celebrating the same, the church and such organizations can unleash a significant volume of encouragement and motivation. This motivation in turn, leads to meaningful performance of leadership roles, healthy leader-member roles, and organizational harmony which itself is a reward, even if no other forms of reward prevail there.

Ministry performance enhancement superstructure, plank 5: communication.

Apart from the general principles governing communication, congregations must be willing to talk not only about triumphs, but disappointments also. They should not view the latter as negative or as pessimism; worse, they should not vilify the leader or member who urges them to consider it. Congregations often do not grieve well for any untoward circumstances apart from death of loved ones. When there are splits, or an exodus of families, or when some other form of church crisis arises, those who stay put and who do not flee the crises by leaving for another church tend to be stoic. They should talk about how they feel; about what they have lost; about what their dreams and disappointments are. By discussing "information about situations that have not worked out so well, you can pass along what you learned from the experience and increase the chances of improving the next time."[17] The church should be the last place where people can't handle the truth, or grow from mistakes; it is what confession and forgiveness are all about, even if as frequently as seventy times seven.[18]

Ministry performance enhancement superstructure, plank 6: setting expectations.

Even though we name this one last, Smith and Mazin identify setting expectations as the first step toward establishing an effective performance management system.[19] Congregations and church organizations should articulate expectations at every level of the entity. Expectations are among the bases of performance evaluation processes; they are the reference point

17. Smith and Mazin, *HR Answer*, 77.
18. Matt 18:15–22.
19. Smith and Mazin, *HR Answer*, 42.

for any measure of accountability. Congregations should not hesitate to hold *all* their members accountable—not only paid staff—especially where infringements, under-performance, mediocrity, and unacceptable service are rendered and are evidently incongruent with set and published expectations. Some congregations fear losing members should they attempt to hold them accountable; but that fear may be exaggerated in many cases. On the contrary, if congregations joyfully and purposefully set expectations, in keeping with their five basic growth goals (personal, spiritual, missional, numerical, and financial) they would set the pace, tone, and parameters for behaviors that correspond with congregational values and excellence. These behaviors, in turn, can only be enhanced with the provision of clear and concise performance management review processes.

Nearly all congregations have an existing ministry enhancement infrastructure; it is in the form of their various congregational and organizational meetings. But infrastructure, by itself, accomplishes little; it needs a superstructure, in the form of a ministry performance enhancement system. Congregations who build that superstructure move toward real performance management. Such performance management is never realized in simply leaving things up to mere meetings, chance, or even "faith."

CONDUCTING A COLLABORATIVE PERFORMANCE REVIEW

A collaborative performance evaluation or review avoids one-sided assessments of persons who might be easily scapegoated or otherwise unfairly targeted in organizations. Churches and church organizations are no exception. The one-sidedness is warded off when the performance review is *collaborative*—meaning that both the targeted worker and the evaluators are equally invested in and are subject to evaluation. The following are crucial steps to follow in setting up a collaborative performance review. While for simplicity, the scenario we imagine below is that of a pastor and congregation—both being evaluated collaboratively—the scenario might, here and there, envisage a multiplicity of organizational staff and people.

Steps toward the review

1. *Set leadership expectations.* Ensure that basic expectations of the pastor's roles are understood by both pastor and congregation. This need not be an exhaustive list; it could, however, include specific areas of pastoral performance which can be categorized into five broad categories for evaluation as follows:

   Quantitative. Did the pastor complete the *numerous* tasks expected of him—preaching, counseling, teaching, visitation, planning, leadership development, and community-building? Did he or she do these in reasonable *frequencies*? Was there a lack in any of these areas? Churches can add other tasks as desired. While they may be tempted to include here such things as the quantitative increase in congregation size or membership, they should desist, as numerical growth (or decrease) of church membership is usually due to a multiplicity of factors, even if it may include the pastor.

   Qualitative. How much impact has the pastor's ministry had, in the period under review, upon the congregation and the community in which the church is situated? Is the congregation hopeful or uneasy; organized or disorganized? Does the congregation enjoy improved or declined health due to the pastor's ministry? Is the congregation challenged or bored? Do the members report signs of spiritual growth, or stagnation or shrinkage, due to the pastor's ministry? To what do they point as proof? While these may also be due to factors other than only the pastor, and while they may indeed be subjective (as qualitative metrics nearly always are), the surveys or questionnaires that ferret out this information from members should seek to be as clear and pointed as possible.

   Organizational compliance. How well has the pastor observed the congregation's best values? (If the congregation does not have a values statement, it should develop one, for the sake of clarity.) To what degree has she or he observed congregational procedures, following the best and healthiest organizational practices? How well has she or he organized or helped organize the church for ministry?

   Relationships. Has the pastor contributed to or forged healthy relationships in the congregation and in the community? Does the pastor's interaction with members encourage productive relationships that strengthen the church's viability in the community, or does she contribute to weakening them? Do reasonable people feel at home in the congregation because of the pastor's approach, or does she push people away?

Expertise and skills. Has the pastor improved his professional skills in the period under review? How well has he utilized, implemented, or demonstrated these skills in the course of this period? Has he made himself more valuable to the organization during this period? Has he shown any kind of creativity or innovation? Has he stimulated new or further vision for the congregation?

2. *Set membership expectations.* Ensure that the congregation understands its roles and what are considered reasonable and basic expectations of them. As with the pastor, whatever these roles and expectations are, they might best be set in broad categories. It is highly recommended that these categories correspond to the pastoral categories, even if the particulars are different. This is necessary for easy collaboration and for the collaborative review. While each congregation is free to insert their own details, the following might apply to most congregations:

Quantitative. What is the percentage of the congregation that supports and cooperates with the pastor to realize and accomplish the congregation's ministry—is it high or low? Does the membership demonstrate reasonably supportive attendance at worship services and meetings? Are they supporting the pastor in the church's ministry to the community? What percentage of the congregation is actively involved in one or more ministry groups or committees of the church?

Qualitative. Does the congregation offer the pastor a healthy environment in which to discharge his ministry? To what degree do they offer opportunities for joy instead of sorrow? Does the congregation exude an aura of healthy spirituality, or, instead, toxicity? Do the members behave in ways that would encourage a new visitor to remain permanently?

Organizational compliance. Do the church's members defend and support the congregation as a *covenant* community, or do they do their own thing and pursue their own agenda? To what degree do members abide by the best values of the congregation? How well do parishioners cooperate with pastor and leaders in organizing the church for ministry?

Relationships. Are members of the congregation genuinely warm with one another and with the pastor? Are members gracious and easy to engage? Are they welcoming and genuinely friendly toward visitors? Does the pastor feel respect and encouragement from leaders and members?

Expertise and skills. Is there any notable effort, from anywhere in the membership, of persons showing deeper interest in leadership development? Are persons offering themselves more intentionally for volunteer positions of service? Have any new skills or gifts been discovered during the period under review?

3. *Establish a review period.* A calendar year or church year may be a suitable period. A year, it should be warned, may be too lengthy a period to go without a performance review. Quarterly may be impractical or feel too frequent for some; a six-month period might be ideal, and is what is recommended here. Especially if personnel changes or rewards and bonuses are offered annually, then a review midway through the period would act as a timely performance enhancer by way of timely feedback for workers who need to adjust their performance one way or another, and for those who need affirmation and encouragement that they are on the right track. It is anything ranging from unhelpful to useless for a worker to hear for the first time, at the end of the review period, where they could have done better during the period. In that case, a mid-period review would have been far better.

4. *Declare the performance period underway.* At the beginning of each new review period, serve personnel with any updated list of expectations. In the case of the congregation, it might be helpful to design a special covenant document that they recite either responsively or in unison, at a special service or the Communion or Eucharist. The church's HR person (or some designated person in the absence of HR) should consider dropping occasional notes or making brief visits to all parties expressing genuine care about how they are doing. Any answers that indicate that some attention might be required should trigger some kind of special and intentional response by the requisite and appropriate partners.

5. *Gather feedback for the collaborative performance review.* Three or four weeks before the review is scheduled to take place, all parties should be apprised of the upcoming review, and reminded of its purpose. In the case of a congregational evaluation along with its pastor, brief surveys should be delivered to them (either hard copy or via an online facility) with simple questions seeking to gauge both their own performance

as a congregation, as well as the pastor's. The questions should closely resemble, answer, and effectively address the five categories identified in Steps 1 and 2. Especially in smaller churches or organizations, the survey might be bypassed if the leaders or a committee are able to adequately gauge what the congregation thinks.

6. *Prepare the collaborative performance review instruments.* Appendices 1 and 2 are instrument models—one for evaluating the congregation, and one for the pastor—by which churches might be guided to construct their own.

7. *Convene the collaborative performance review meeting.* Appendix 3 is a document that guides the review meeting.

Performance matters. If there is to be any excellence in ministry and if church organizations are to pursue a more perfect condition, they should embrace measures that enable staff and people—leaders and followers—to develop better practices and improve performance.

Chapter 11

Evaluating the Church's Programs

CHURCH PEOPLE, CHURCH INSTITUTIONS, and their organizations, which do not desire to be led into dysfunction, should be always committed to honest and timely evaluation of as many of their functions, programs, and initiatives as possible. No healthy organization should wish to proceed for very long without taking some kind of inventory of its progress. One of those inventories is of their programs, specifically regarding their effectiveness, efficiency, outcomes, value, benefits, and more. A fair criticism of many faith-based organizations—especially churches—is that because they trust the Holy Spirit's power, and assume that God would bless their efforts and honor them when they, God's people, honor God, they seldom evaluate their ministries. Some even cite an intriguing episode in the life of King David, where he counted his troops and annoyed God[1] as biblical proof that taking inventories, taking stock, measuring results, and evaluating programs are all sinful. There are those, of course, who would be adamant that this is a gross misinterpretation of scriptures and poor hermeneutics.

It would be most certainly a journey toward dysfunction if a church, church organization, or denominational organization, were to forge ahead with programs that they never evaluated. Evaluation is one matter; the nature, quality, and extent of evaluations are another. The objective of this chapter is to offer steps that should be included in a meaningful and effective program evaluation process, and some of the best practices toward that end.

But why program evaluation? If the answer were to be reduced to one single reason, it would be this: until a church's program is properly evaluated, things might be farther from reality—unlike images in the rearview mirror—than they appear to be. Instead, failure may be nearer than it

---

1. See 2 Sam 24 and 1 Chr 21.

appears to be (like the danger in the rearview mirror)! In the rare case, the program may no longer be addressing its objectives because it has *already* done so, its success completed, and a new program addressing a new target may be long overdue.

THE CASE OF THE CRESTVIEW COMMUNITY CHURCH

By virtue of her 4,000 strong membership and a weekly attendance of more than 2,000, the Crestview Community Church (hereinafter referred to as "Crestview") is one of the city of Sigmund's megachurches. A congregation which ordinarily hosts about 2,000 attendees weekly is widely considered a megachurch. Located in North Sigmund, the ninety-two-year-old congregation is under the pastoral leadership of Gregory Cruickshank, who has been at the helm for a dozen years. Until now, only a fraction of America's churches are megachurches. It is therefore still a remarkable development for a single congregation to have so many members and draw, weekly, such a large number of worshipers. Crestview is even more remarkable in that it is the only megachurch of African-American vintage in Sigmund *and* in the entire state!

Crestview conducts a weekly event called the Deeper Growth Ministry. Although this is only one component of Crestview's Discipleship and Christian Education Ministry, it is clearly intended to be Crestview's signature discipleship development ministry.[2] Stephen Porter, Crestview's Pastor of Discipleship, embraces the vision that all of Crestview's four thousand members who are able-bodied, and who attend worship weekly, ought to be involved in the discipleship ministry. Porter offers the illustration that while a baby is born through the facilitation of an obstetrician, the growing child needs the attention of—not an obstetrician—but a pediatrician. He does this to illustrate a growing Christian's need for *discipleship*—not merely *conversion*—beyond the basic claims of the faith. Porter is concerned about the development of Crestview's members in discipleship; as well he should be. This megachurch's weekly attendance at Deeper Growth Ministry classes averaged 122 in 2013—a mere 3 percent of Crestview's membership, and under 5 percent of weekly attendance. This was the lowest in five years, and the third successive year of a slow downward trend.[3]

2. There are five other components of the broader ministry, according to a Crestview Ministry Work Plan document viewed by this evaluator/author.

3. Source: Crestview's Deeper Growth Ministry Report, presented at the Ministry's monthly meeting on January 25, 2014.

These facts and concerns led Porter, along with this author, to pursue an evaluation of Crestview's Deeper Growth Ministry (hereinafter referred to, often, as DGM), with a view to understanding the ministry's progress, problems, and potential. The intent of the evaluation was also to gauge how viable and desirable the ministry is to Crestview's members; and if at all considered valuable, whether there may be any ways in which the ministry might be improved and engage more of Crestview's members.

In order to review Crestview's DGM, several steps were followed. We itemize each of these steps below. Readers desirous of developing a program evaluation may follow these steps.

TEN STEPS IN PROGRAM EVALUATION

1. *Observe your organization's realities and believe what they are telling you.* Look at evident realities, evident facts, and evident statistics, and believe what you see. In some cases, actual and clear data may be available (as with Crestview's membership vis-à-vis their DGM attendance). In some other cases, little or no data may be as evident. Take, for example, Oldbury Church (the museum) which we saw in chapter 1. Each year, Oldbury has what they call an evangelistic campaign—a "crusade"—into which they pour a lot of money and a lot of energy. The church baptizes a number of persons, many requesting baptism as a result of these crusades. However, Oldbury sees no overall increase in Sunday attendance; on the contrary, they have seen a continual decrease in their Wednesday evening Bible Study meeting, aimed at discipleship for both mature—and especially new—Christians, and their Sunday attendance at both services has declined dramatically.

   In Crestview's case, it may be easy to relate measurable DGM attendance to overall membership as a clue for exploring the effectiveness of the DGM. But how does one measure spirituality or true conversion, *statistically*? In Oldbury's case, they may not be able to measure either of these from simply the attendance figures seen on Sundays or Wednesdays. However, observing the fact that their two most vital signs (attendance on Sundays and Wednesdays) have nosedived, Oldbury may theorize that some kind of disconnect exists between crusades and discipleship. That theory, in turn, could lead Oldbury's leaders to do a much-needed program evaluation of anything, ranging between their annual evangelistic campaigns to their program of integrating the baptized into the church's life, or even as far as the effectiveness of the church's entire ministry. Oldbury should believe that the lack of life around them is telling the truth. They should then do something about it, beginning with a program evaluation.

2. *Seek agreement among key leaders that a program evaluation is necessary.* It is essential that all key leaders be on board with an evaluation; if not, the project is either likely to fail, or would not otherwise be embraced and implemented right through to the end. In the specific case of Crestview, their DGM evaluation was completed, up to the point of reliable findings and solid recommendations. The objective of an evaluation, however, is not merely reliable findings; it is the *implementation* of suggestions and recommendations arising from the reliable findings. In Crestview's case, this author had always perceived a measure of distance and disinterest on the part of Crestview's senior pastor, despite his agreement to the evaluation being done. Even though Porter, the discipleship pastor, gave his utmost assistance and support; even though the DGM's leaders and teachers all cooperated; even though over one hundred of Crestview's members completed surveys, the failure of the church to implement the evaluation's crucial recommendations was due chiefly (and perhaps solely), to the senior pastor's disengagement.

3. *Secure a program evaluator.* Depending on the need, a program evaluator need not be a professional evaluator; it can be someone from within the congregation with the requisite skills and time for research and evaluation. While objectivity could be somewhat a challenge with someone from the congregation, the plus side is that someone who knows the congregation might have a better sense of what to examine, what to question, what to look for, and who to interview. A trained and competent evaluator though, would still be the greater advantage; in this circumstance, the objectivity and dispassionate distance that such a person brings to the project may be the organization's best friend. Once the evaluator has been secured, Steps 4 through 9 are that person's remit and responsibility. Step 10 is for the program's managers and the church organization.

4. *Do a literature review.* A valid program evaluation involves a reasonable measure of research beyond the immediate program itself. It requires an understanding of the broader context of programs like itself,

including other people, churches, and organizations' experience with similar programs. It requires, in the case of a church organization, some investigation into the theology that undergirds or supposedly undergirds either the program itself, or which might reasonably be considered the congregation's premise for launching the program in the first place. The nature of the program being evaluated would determine the literature that is sourced and secured. The literature search—even before the review—is itself investigative; the evaluator should try to be as exhaustive and creative as possible, because of the wealth of information that is already likely to exist regarding the issue. In the case of Crestview church's DGM, the following crucial issues led the evaluator to select certain materials: (a) changes in church attendance patterns; (b) the congregation as the location of discipleship development; (c) developing disciples beyond ordinary church meetings and events; (d) new ways and formats of teaching the Bible in church; (e) consumerism issues especially in megachurches; and (f) current trends in church people's understanding of membership, and expectations and requirements of membership. Each one of these six broad issues supplied, in turn, a variety of subordinate leads. Consequently, the final list of materials gathered for a literature review was extensive, and reflective of these concerns. The literature review is not just a reading exercise; evaluators are looking for, noting, and cataloguing clues within the literature that enable them to pursue leads that reveal truths about the program they are investigating and evaluating.

5. *Formulate a research question and determine a methodology.* It is recommended that researchers discover what program managers think would improve efficiency.[4] Program evaluators, then, should make that discovery a major part of the objective of their research, attempting at every point to determine what stakeholders (some of whom, in our example, are Crestview's members) might see as able to assist with service delivery,[5] and to examine among stakeholders the perception of need.[6] The research question may not necessarily be a single question. The evaluator may have to ask herself several related questions that would guide the research. The usual questions might be: What is wrong with this program? Why is it not achieving its desired goals? What can be

4. Posavac, *Program Evaluation*, 96.
5. Ibid., 97.
6. Ibid., 108.

done to improve this program or the people's participation? Is this program even needed? Can it be done differently or scheduled at a different time? What other programs or supporting systems is this program dependent upon? Is there a systemic problem in the organization, broader than the program under review?

Regarding methodology, the four major approaches which were adopted in Crestview's case should be among the most crucial that an evaluator of any congregation or church organization's program should adopt: (1) interviews with key parties in the program under review (in this case, Crestview's pastors, DGM leaders and staff, and notably outstanding attendees); (2) non-participant observation of the program in progress, action, and delivery (in this case, attending DGM classes and staff meetings over an extensive period of time); (3) examination of any program or parent organization's documents that might provide crucial information, insight, and leads toward better evaluating the program (in this case, *all* of Crestview church's documents—constitution, bylaws, brochures, magazines, bulletins, and more—as well as all of their DGM documents; and (4) a survey or surveys using the program's participants as the sample.

6. *Execute the methodology.* Conduct interviews with the targeted persons. Attend every meeting of the program as far as possible—both the planning meetings and the actual meetings or events where the program is delivered. Observe silently sometimes. Ask questions sometimes. Learn. Note your impressions. Watch people carefully. Allow a generous period of time (several weeks in most cases might be the standard) for this step. Gather the organization and program's documents, as many as you would be allowed; insist on having even what might be considered sensitive documents which might be relevant to the program. Prepare the survey or surveys. Deliver the surveys (whether online or hard copies). Receive the completed surveys. Collate and analyze the survey information.

7. *Get to work with the information supplied from both the literature review and the methodology.* After careful analysis, the evaluator should be able to write a cogent paper that leads to a number of theological, sociological, and ideological results and findings and which can provide the congregation, or the program's planners and managers, opportunities for discussion. (Again, depending on the organization's need, the evaluator need not be someone necessarily schooled

in any of those disciplines.) In other words, before jumping to what to do or change, the evaluator brings to the fore, ideas and values that would supply the proper framework for what to do. In Crestview's case, where a 4,000 member church saw only 122 participants in their weekly discipleship classes, the evaluator arrived at these four values: (a) the *incubator* of discipleship—that the congregation is the locus of discipleship development; (b) the *imperative* of discipleship—that discipleship development is necessary in and for the congregation; (c) *innovations* with discipleship—that Bible teaching and discipleship development is happening elsewhere in new ways with tremendous success, even in megachurches, and that Crestview could learn a thing or two from them; (d) the *ideology* of discipleship—is it, for Crestview members, a matter of consumerism or commitment?

8. *Summarize your observations and recommendations.* Whatever the broader ideological, theological, or sociological framework and ideas might be, the evaluator now has enough materials and experience with the program so as to enable the summarization of her observations and recommendations to the program's managers.

9. *Invite the program's managers, leaders and key people to a meeting.* It would be better for the evaluator's findings to be delivered in a meeting where discussion could ensue. A meeting of the key persons is expected to be significantly more helpful than simply the delivery of the written report to persons by hand or by mail, and leaving the rest up to chance. That would be tantamount to—even after all of that work—leading the program and its church organization into dysfunction.

10. *Accept, discuss, modify, and adopt the program evaluator's recommendations.* This step may happen over a period of time spanning more than one meeting. It should be done in a spirit of joy and expectancy. If the measures require retiring the entire program or some part thereof, it should be done with dignity and in the context of a service of dismissal that celebrates what God has done over the years when it was in effect. Perhaps a few of the program's alumni might be invited to offer testimonies of how the program blessed and developed their lives. Should not what the program did for them be considered a positive part of the evaluation also?

Often, however, a program evaluation, instead of leading to the retiring of the program, may lead to action that requires a strategic plan to execute something better. That is the focus of the next chapter.

PART IV

So Much Spirit, So Little Strategy!

Strategy without tactics is the slowest route to victory. Tactics without strategy is the noise before defeat.

—*Sun Tzŭ*

Suppose one of you wants to build a tower. Will he not first sit down and estimate the cost to see if he has enough money to complete it? For if he lays the foundation and is not able to finish it, everyone who sees it will ridicule him, saying, "This fellow began to build and was not able to finish."

—*Luke 14:28–30, NIV*

Or suppose a king is about to go to war against another king. Will he not first sit down and consider whether he is able with ten thousand men to oppose the one coming against him with twenty thousand?

—*Luke 14:31, NIV*

Chapter 12

Building a Strategic Plan for Your Church

THE CHURCH IS A spiritual entity; there are some, so convinced that this is the only nature of the church, who therefore find it difficult to admit that the church is also an organization. But alas, even congregations that are considered to be the holiest and most spiritual of entities *do* fall into a state of dysfunction. While persons may be ready to blame other persons for the dysfunction of any church that understands itself as an organization too, one is certain that nobody would dare to blame the Spirit for dysfunction in a church considered spiritual! Who or what, then, is the culprit? The answer is the people who lead and participate in such churches. Some dysfunctional churches can feel quite devoid of the Spirit. On the other hand, some dysfunctional churches may be full of the Spirit—they are nice people (humble, kind, teachable, and faithful, and peace reigns in the church between members) but the church has either plateaued in many areas where growth should be expected, or is declining. Why? It might be that the church may have spirit, but little strategy. Church people, church institutions, and their organizations, which do not desire to be led into dysfunction, should pursue strategic thinking and procedures as committedly as they pursue spiritual growth.

The church's primary objective, one might assert, is transformation—transformation of individual lives, of entire communities of faith, of civil, social, and national communities, and even of the world. Transformation rarely happens by chance. It requires strategy: strategic thinking, planning, and positioning. Unfortunately, as indispensable as spirit is to the church, spirit is neither enough, nor truly divine, if it lacks strategy. Even Jesus embraced strategy. He could not imagine a builder not counting the cost and requirements for constructing a tower; nor could he envisage a wartime general going to battle without a strategy.[1]

In the last chapter, we used the experience of Crestview Community Church to illustrate the steps in completing a program evaluation. In this chapter, we return to Crestview as the example, in demonstrating how one might develop a strategic plan for one's church or one of its programs. After evaluating Crestview's Deeper Growth Ministry (DGM), a strategic plan was developed to address the problems discovered and explored in their program evaluation. Simply put, wherever the church or a church organization finds a significant problem therein, a strategic plan may be the most effective means of addressing the problem.

It might be recalled that, despite its weekly attendance exceeding 2,000, Crestview Community Church averaged 122 in attendance in 2013 in their Deeper Growth Ministry (DGM) program—the congregation's signature discipleship development ministry and program. The evaluation of this ministry found that, though so poorly attended, the program is valuable and viable, but required many significant adjustments. Because Crestview, with a 4,000 strong membership, is committed to making disciples, and because the DGM is a cornerstone of this commitment, a 3 percent DGM attendance statistic highlights the palpable need and challenge for a significantly improved attendance, and the fulfillment of Crestview's overall objective of making disciples. This chapter shall refer to Crestview's pursuit of a strategic plan to address its own DGM, as an example for any congregation, denomination, or church organization that desires to address its own needs and challenges. In Crestview's case, their strategic plan offers clear and concrete steps toward realizing the need for moving attendance at DGM classes from 6 percent of weekly *attendance* in 2013, to 50 percent over the period of thirty months.

FIFTEEN STEPS TOWARD AN EFFECTIVE STRATEGIC PLAN

1. *Identify the problem or the objective that requires a strategic plan.* Strategic plans do not appear out of thin air. The need for a strategic plan usually arises from one of two stimuli: either a significant problem that the organization wants to address with a plan to manage it, or a

1. Luke 14:28–33.

significant objective that requires a strategy to realize it. We say "significant" because strategic plans usually are not required for simple or minor problems or objectives.

2. *Select a strategic planning team.* The best strategic plans are not the product of a one-man show. So, gather a competent and committed team of people who are exercised by the challenge of the problem that demands a new strategy, and who are energized by the prospects ahead, that are enshrined in the objective already chosen or due to be discovered. This team should include persons—stakeholders—who are deeply interested in the issue at hand, and ready and able to undertake its analysis, if not also its execution.

3. *The team should familiarize itself with the organizational history of the organizational parent.* Always go a step above the particular item or entity being targeted for a strategic plan. For example, if a strategic plan is being developed for a denomination, investigate the history of the international denomination; if it is for a congregation, begin with the national or regional denomination; and if it is for a program in the congregation, begin with the congregation itself. (The latter was the approach taken with Crestview's DGM, wherein the church—not just the DGM—was studied.) Investigate, understand, and appreciate the entity's values, vision, and mission statements. If none exists, as challenging as it might be, attempt to discern what might be their values, vision, and mission. All of this enables the development of a reasonable profile of the organization which would, in turn, enable a better command of strategic planning for the entity within the parent organization.

In the case of Crestview, it was essential to discover that the church's four-fold mission statement committed the church to (a) lift up Jesus, (b) reach the unchurched, (c) empower believers, and (d) widen God's kingdom.[2] A three-fold pastoral vision statement which shares as much prominence and visibility as the mission statement, invites Crestview to (a) pay off their mortgage, (b) maintain their properties, and (c) develop leaders.[3] Both of these statements clarify and amplify the fact that discipleship is a prominent Crestview value, evident in the clauses, *empowering believers* and *develop leaders*.

2. Crestview's weekly Sunday bulletin displays this statement.
3. Ibid.

Further, Crestview's Work Plan for Discipleship[4] declares that "it is the primary purpose of the Discipleship and Christian Education Ministry is [sic] to help Crestview . . . Church members to grow spiritually by developing new membership converts into disciples, and disciples into kingdom servants and servant leaders."[5] Then, too, Crestview's DGM Brochure with the course/class offerings declares that "the Deeper Growth Ministry is not just a supplemental ministry within the congregation; it is a vital component of the Great Commission left by Jesus commanding us to teach disciples to obey all that He has commanded."[6]

If it were only Crestview's DGM documents that were investigated and not the parent organization's (Crestview), some of this indispensable information, with direct implications for and bearings on the DGM would have been overlooked; and the strategic plan would have been weakened from the start. From these crucial Crestview documents, Crestview's evident and high value on discipleship development demanded that, in the wake of an abysmal 3 percent attendance at a church ministry called *life* development, a strategic plan had to be developed to bring Crestview's behavior in sync with its values. So a strategic plan was designed to accomplish precisely that: to pursue the high, healthy, happy, and holy vision of realizing, within a two year period, a weekly attendance of 1,000 at Life Development Classes, instead of 122—a goal which would equal 25 percent of membership or 50 percent of weekly attendance.

4. *Develop either a problem tree or an objective tree.* If you begin with an objective that is already stated, you will need an objective tree; likewise, if you begin with a problem, you will need a problem tree. Problem and objective trees are investigative and strategic planning techniques that analyze a problem or an objective, respectively. As the name implies, the tree has a trunk, roots, and branches. The trunk is the presenting problem or objective, which has sparked the need for a strategic plan. In Crestview's case, it is a problem that is analyzed. Their problem is the fact that only 3 percent of their membership are utilizing the DGM, which is Crestview's signature program for

4. This is another unpublished Crestview document, governing the DGM for 2014–2015.

5. Ibid, 3.

6. Crestview Church's Deeper Growth Ministry (Sunday School) Brochure.

discipleship development. The roots of the tree are those things that have *caused* the problem. The program evaluation that Crestview did and which we visited in the last chapter, revealed many of the deeper problems that have caused the DGM to be so poorly attended. Attempting to develop a strategic plan without a prior program evaluation is the certain road to disaster at worst and fogginess at best; it is a road that quickly leads to dysfunction. Then, the branches in the problem tree are the effects the presenting problem is likely to produce if the problem is not fixed. If you are launching a strategic plan to address some problem, chances are that many of that problem's effects are already unfolding. A problem tree that is developed in a meeting of the strategic planning team can be an exciting and inspiring exercise, even though it is a problem that is being addressed. This is so because within the problem tree are the seeds of hope, remedy, restoration, and clues for what needs to be undertaken in the new strategy. Crestview's problem tree is illustrated in Figure 6.

Crestview's Problem Tree

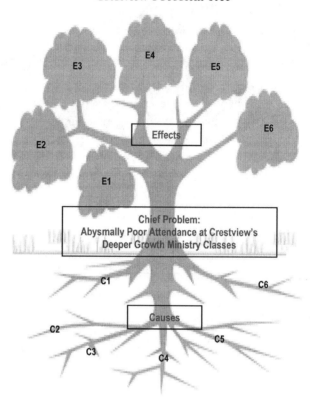

Key
C1 – C6 are the six *causes* of the chief problem.
E1 – E6 are the six *effects* of the chief problem.

C1 Ill-equipped teaching staff and ineffective teaching.
C2 Inadequate promotion of the DGM in worship by leaders.
C3 Poor example set by leaders who don't attend DGM.
C4 The DGM isn't promoted as crucial for Crestview's life and development.
C5 More attention, resources spent on worship and music.
C6 The DGM is not assessed adequately or regularly.

E1 Frustrated teachers; frustration leaks to students.
E2 The DGM is perceived as non-essential by Crestviewers.
E3 Crestview's members become under-developed disciples.
E4 Crestview becomes an under-developed church.
E5 Crestview, strong in worship, is weak in discipleship.
E6 The DGM continues a downward spiral to ineffectiveness.

Figure 6

If it were an objective tree that were used to address Crestview's needs, the trunk of the tree would be the objective (or desired result), the roots would be the means to achieve that objective, and the branches would be the outcome or ends at which the means all aim. Crestview's objective tree is illustrated in Figure 7.

Crestview's Objective Tree

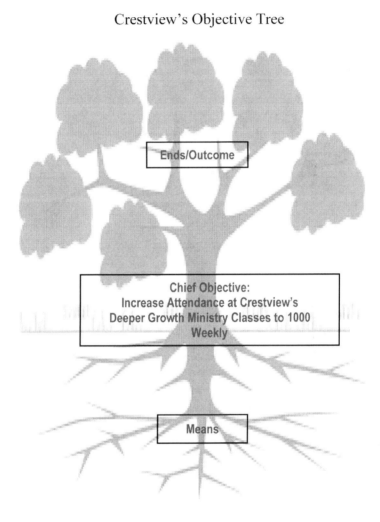

Ends/Outcome

Chief Objective:
Increase Attendance at Crestview's
Deeper Growth Ministry Classes to 1000
Weekly

Means

Figure 7

5. *Summarize the core issue.* In the case of a problem tree, state clearly what the problem is, itemize what the causes are, and itemize what

the effects are. (The same principle applies for an objective tree: state clearly what the objective is, itemize what the means are, and itemize what the ends/outcomes are.) In Crestview's case, the problem was summarized as "abysmally low attendance at Deeper Growth Ministry classes." The causes beneath these problems (identified during the previous program evaluation) included ill-equipped teaching staff, ineffective teaching, inadequate resources spent on developing the program, and more. Two major effects, among others, are that Crestview members become underdeveloped, undisciplined, ineffective, and non-exemplary disciples; and that Crestview becomes an underdeveloped church denying its own value of discipleship.

6. *Complete a stakeholder analysis.* All stakeholder segments (comprising persons who make impact upon, or upon whom impact is made by the program or entity for which the strategic plan is being developed) should be analyzed, specifically to determine their level of interest in the problem being addressed in relation to their power to change anything about it. This analysis would give the strategic team leads about where to invest energy, to whom responsibilities should be given, and around or with whom to navigate certain aspects of the plan. The persons with high levels of interest may have low power, and the persons with high power may have low interest. So the aim of the stakeholder analysis is to determine who, if any, has both high interest and high power—the perfect combination. In Crestview's case, six categories of persons were considered concerned parties, or parties which ought to have been concerned with Crestview's problem of abysmally low attendance at DGM classes. These persons—otherwise known as stakeholders—were as follows: pastors, deacons, trustees, DGM teachers, DGM attendees, non-DGM attendees (especially potential attendees), and the public at large, who make up the society in which Crestview's disciples are meant to make a difference. Crestview's stakeholder analysis is illustrated in Figure 8.

Crestview's Stakeholder Analysis

Stakeholder Prioritizing Quadrant:
The four quadrants organize Crestview's Deeper Growth Ministry stakeholders (interest parties) according to **Interest** (the *horizontal* axis, where left is low, and right is high) and **Power** (the *vertical* axis, where top is high and bottom is low).

	High Power, Low Interest	High Power, High Interest
P O W E R	Senior Pastor Trustees Deacons	Associate Pastor DGM Teachers & Leaders
	Low Power, Low Interest	**Low Power, High Interest**
	Non-attending Members Sigmund's Public-at-Large	Students (DGM Attendees)

◄⸻⸻⸻ **INTEREST** ⸻⸻⸻►

Stakeholder Analysis Findings:
(1) Crestview's Associate Pastor and Deeper Growth Ministry Teachers and Leaders have high power to affect the program for better or worse; they also have high interest in the ministry.
(2) Crestview's current Deeper Growth Ministry Attendees have, obviously, high interest in the ministry, but are not decision-makers about the program, although their opinions could, should, and have been sought.
(3) Crestview's Senior Pastor, Trustees and Deacons have power, high enough to determine whether Crestview's budget starves or saves the Deeper Growth Ministry, and high enough to send a powerful message to Crestview's masses that either the DGM is a waste of time or a crucial and invaluable Christian need. But alas! These powerful leaders have low interest in the DGM. The fact that Crestview's Senior Pastor has low interest signals a major problem with successfully rectifying Crestview's chief problem.
(4) Crestview's non-attending-DGM members possess the same low interest as if they were the non-member Public-at-Large. Due to their distance, their power is also low.

Figure 8

7. *Complete a situational analysis.* Situational analyses come in various forms. As the name implies, they enable realistic assessments of one's environment and current organizational situation. The most commonly known is the SWOT analysis: S for strengths, W for weaknesses, O for opportunities, and T for threats. The strategic planning team asks itself questions about each, regarding their own organization or organizational program. Another slightly different approach is a SOAR analysis: S for strengths, O for opportunities, A for aspirations, and R for results—the results if the aspirations are realized. This was the format used for Crestview. While there may be some danger in removing focus

from threats, a benefit in SOAR is that it intentionally trains the strategic plan team toward the future, by looking at aspirations. A team is free to do a combination of these two approaches, or others as desired.

8. *Develop the core strategy.* Having undertaken Steps 1 through 6 above, the team is now able to formulate a succinct, chief, and overarching strategy for execution. The strategy begins with a very clear strategic goal that answers the question: what exactly are we going to set out to do? Crestview's strategic goal was to increase enrollment in and attendance at Crestview Community Church's Deeper Growth Ministry Classes to 1,000 participants weekly, by the end of the ensuing thirty months. The strategy continues through to Step 13.

9. *Evaluate what could be lost should the strategy not be executed.* While this might seem unnecessary, sometimes, after all the work is done and a strategic plan developed, no execution takes place. What can be lost and what opportunities missed can offer motivation for the organization's leaders to ensure that the plan is executed. Crestview understood that, should they not pursue their strategic plan as outlined, it is certain that Crestview would not turn their problem around. They understood further that if they did not turn this problem around, they may face not only a credibility crisis, but also an identity crisis: a credibility crisis, in that it would not be able to defend its claim to be a church that turns members into disciples; and an identity crisis, in that Crestview would be effectively repudiating its own values, vision, and mission as a congregation.

10. *Evaluate what could be gained should the strategy be executed.* The achievement of the strategic goal is one thing; but its ripple effects, implications, and possibilities are quite another. It is important to note the possibilities *beyond* the strategic goal so that the organization might understand that it is not an end in itself, and is a contributor to the wider purpose of usefulness in the world beyond itself. In other words, a strategic goal is to be understood as only a small part of something bigger and beyond the organization's own self. When the church, denomination or church organization understands itself as only part of a larger narrative, it might be inclined to take its strategic objectives much more urgently. In the case of Crestview, were they to move their DGM attendance from 3 percent of membership to 25 percent in thirty months, then it might be expected that Crestview may be able

to repeat or continue this process to aim at increasing enrollment even beyond 25 percent of membership (one thousand), to more and more of membership, in the years beyond the two-and-a-half envisaged in their strategic plan. Additionally, Crestview may become, later on, a model for her regional, national, or international denominational family; their influence could extend beyond denominational boundaries, because churches elsewhere may be encouraged to copy their strategy, or imitate them. Should this happen, Crestview could find that they contributed to the encouragement of Christians far away, and even began a global movement. When a local strategic goal is understood as having implications for a bigger stage, that strategy may take wings and invite a greater urgency from its planners and executors.

11. *Outline the strategic plan's goals.* First, state the *general* goal. The general goal is the one alluded to in Step 10; it is the overall, wider accomplishment in the world to which the strategic goal being pursued by your team might contribute greatly. Second, restate your *strategic* goal, as outlined before, in Step 7. In order to gather the wider membership's input and wisdom, this might be a good time to develop and distribute surveys and questionnaires and to conduct interviews. Information from Steps 6 and 7 (the stakeholder and situational analyses, respectively) can supply intelligence for these surveys, questionnaires and interviews, enabling the team to know whom to ask what. Results from these would, in turn, offer many leads for Step 12.

12. *Outline the strategic plan's objectives.* The objectives itemize and unpack the variety of implications in and actions required to achieve the strategic goal. The objectives answer the question: what do we need to do to reach this strategic goal? Crestview's component objectives included actions such as increasing the DGM teaching staff, equipping and improving teaching skills for DGM staff, better promotion of the DGM during worship, devoting more resources toward developing the DGM, adding a variety of new meeting times and places to accommodate the larger enrollment, and doing regular evaluations of the DGM ministry. Each objective should be SMART: "S" for specific, "M" for measurable, "A" for achievable, "R" for realistic, and "T" for time sensitive. Other metrics such as CLEAR might be considered also: "C" for collaborative, "L" for limited, "E" for emotional, "A" for appreciable, and "R" for refinable.

13. *Outline the implementation.* In order for a strategic goal to be accomplished, several actions in a timely manner are required. Itemize each step to be taken, in a logical and chronological order, and apply a time frame to each. Using the list of objectives already outlined, actual tasks for stakeholders should be delineated—tasks to accomplish each objective. A budgetary component to this step is necessary, so a budget should be drafted. When done, this step should clearly outline task, doers, completion dates, and budgetary requirements.

    Some strategic planners find a logical framework matrix to be a useful technique for laying out the implementation, while some others find it to be a distraction. Logical framework matrices begin by naming the *activities* to be implemented. Those acts are tested for their *performance indicators* (how shall one *know* they have been completed?), for their *means of verification* (how shall one *show* that they have been completed?) and for the *chief assumptions* about the results of their implementation. Only when the activities are satisfactorily tested do the planners go upward to the *component objectives* (which the activities are meant to complete). These are tested, similarly, by the same criteria of performance indicators, means of verification, and assumptions. After the component objectives are satisfactorily tested, the planners go upward again, to the *specific program objective* (the strategic goal), testing it as the other items before. When that goal is satisfactorily and logically tested, it gives way to the general goal. Crestview's logical framework matrix can be viewed in Appendix 4.

14. *Develop an evaluation plan.* It is highly recommended that neither the strategic team, nor the congregation or church organization's leaders, depend only on the outcome or the accomplishment of the strategic goal to determine anything about the success of the plan. Because of this, an evaluation plan should be part of the strategic plan. In order to pursue meaningful evaluation of a strategic plan, one should "clearly define and articulate the linkages between the organization's mission, vision, goals, strategies, programs, and measures."[7] Further, "an integrated system of performance measures is no substitute for a compelling mission, uplifting vision, clear goals, and innovative strategies."[8] Evaluations go past results (defined as the outcomes of what was actually done) to something much broader: *impact.* Impact is understood

---

7. Sawhill and Williamson, "Mission Impossible?" 374.
8. Ibid., 385.

as the effect of the strategic goal's completion, long after it has been completed, and beyond the immediate satisfaction that the goal has been reached. Impact looks for levels of satisfaction or dissatisfaction among all stakeholders, long after the strategic goal has been reached. The strategic team needs to devise a system by which this evaluation might be undertaken. The evaluator is likely to take a look at each of the stakeholder/actor categories which were expected to contribute to some aspect of the execution of the strategic plan.

15. *Appoint a strategic plan executor.* While the strategic team might be considered the best operatives to execute the strategic plan, in some cases it may not be either possible or wise. Regardless of who would execute the plan, it would be helpful for the strategic plan to indicate the wisdom of selecting an executor who oversees the implementation of the strategic plan and is accountable to the church board or council or organization's leaders. The executor's work, since it would involve regular contact and meetings with stakeholders who execute various component objectives, shall—if well-documented—contribute greatly to the evaluation due after the plan has been executed. The strategic plan executor should be completely committed to the strategic plan, and to the faith community's vision, values, and mission. He or she must have the requisite discipline for executing the steps outlined in the plan. In the context of a faith community, he or she should be prayerfully given the authority and clearance to convene the meetings and complete the administrative necessities that would facilitate both the execution of the strategic plan, as well as the evaluation of this plan.

Chapter 13

Epilogue: Whom Do Churches Lead?

> He went to Nazareth, where he had been brought up, and on the Sabbath day he went into the synagogue, as was his custom. And he stood up to read. The scroll of the prophet Isaiah was handed to him. Unrolling it, he found the place where it is written: "The Spirit of the Lord is on me, because he has anointed me to preach good news to the poor. He has sent me to proclaim freedom for the prisoners and recovery of sight for the blind, to release the oppressed, to proclaim the year of the Lord's favor." Then he rolled up the scroll, gave it back to the attendant and sat down. The eyes of everyone in the synagogue were fastened on him, and he began by saying to them, "Today this scripture is fulfilled in your hearing."[1]

THE CHRISTIAN BIBLE HAS been subjected to a variety of interpretations over the ages. Among the interpretations are some of the misnomers for which church people have a penchant. There is a section we call the "Shepherd's Psalm," but in truth, it is the sheep's psalm, since it is the sheep who is writing and speaking. There is a passage we call "The Lord's Prayer," although it is really the disciples' prayer, or more correctly, *lessons* on prayer; for the Lord's Prayer is better located in John 17. There is still another which we have called "The Parable of the Good Samaritan," as though—using the definite article—all other Samaritans are or were bad! We use the definite article, once more, in reference to Matt 28:18–20, which we call "The Great Commission," as though there is only one. We contend here that there is more than one. We assert that Luke 4:16–21, too, is to be understood as *a* great commission—firstly, for Jesus, and ultimately, for Jesus's followers.

---

1. Luke 4:16–21.

There can be no doubt that when Jesus publicly stood, read, and then declared fulfillment of what he had just read, he was announcing, as it were, his manifesto for his ministry. In Luke's gospel, Jesus's approach to ministry is radical like nowhere else. He touches the untouchables—whether inflicted with mental, emotional, or spiritual depression, leprosy, or paralysis, or blindness (Luke 4:31–37; 5:12–26; 17:11–19; 18:35–40). He relieves the needy from the rigor of misapplied law and the miscarriage of justice (6:1–11; 13:10–17). He practically inducts women into the hallowed halls of learning that were exclusively set aside for men, liberating women from the stereotypical domestication expected of them (10:38–41). Women, girls and children are upheld as worthy of their rightful place in society, no less valuable than men (7:36–50; 8:40–56; 13:10–17; 18:15–17; 21:1–4). Jesus elevates a hated race to the same level of dignity as a supposedly chosen race, and in fact applies greater honor to the hated race (10:25–37). He acknowledges the value and human dignity of those forgotten by society, never considered for any honor, recognition, or celebration (14:15–24). He turns justice on its head, elevating mercy, love, forgiveness, and welcome as necessary for true justice (15:11–32). He demonstrates both the short-term and the long-term negative impact of social injustice, greed, imbalance of wealth distribution, and human suffering, showing that the privileged may not be as safe and secure as they might think (16:19–31). At the same time, he warns the rich about selfishness and the danger of being controlled and imprisoned by their riches (18:18–30). The need for justice to prevail in human society (18:1–8; 19:1–10) is of utmost concern as Jesus selects Isaiah's scroll that awesome and fateful day.

Let us be clear: Jesus took sides. It is not that he ignored the powerful Pharisees; for he did accept an invitation for dinner at a Pharisee's home. Neither did he reject the rich; for one of his twelve was a tax collector, and he invited a rich young businessman to follow him (although the invitation was refused). But the burden of Jesus's ministry was—as he declared in his manifesto—a focus on the poor, the imprisoned, the blind, the oppressed, and a system desperately in need of constant and perpetual jubilee. Lev 25:8–55 outlines the conditions for the Year of Jubilee, occurring once every fifty years. It is to be a year governed and characterized by generosity, forgiveness of debts, cancelation of burdens, and restoration of original land ownership rights. It includes relief for the poor, the outcast, the alien, and the dispossessed. Jesus's intention as he read Isaiah was to declare perpetual jubilee. Jesus, as he announced his manifesto, declared therein his values, vision, and mission—those three indispensable parts of leadership DNA. This, therefore, was how Jesus led. It is to be understood as the model to which any Jesus-follower should subscribe for a pattern. It must be the church's pattern for leadership, and leadership engagement in the world.

When all is said and done, leadership within congregations, or denominations, or church and denominational organizations, is all well and good when such entities are energized with whatever they determine to be good leadership. But what is all of that leadership for? What is a healthy congregation or denomination or church organization to *do* with their health? What must they now lead? Who must they now lead? The answer is clear: if they shall follow Jesus, the church must lead the ministry of justice in the world, focusing on the poor, the imprisoned, the blind, the oppressed, and pursuing in their world the constant and perpetual jubilee which was the ministry of Jesus. The church's people must hold this great commission as dearly and as equally as they hold the other great commission which, hitherto, they may have considered to be the *only* great commission. Indeed, it should not be difficult to see how Jesus, in making disciples himself—which he commands his followers to do—did it as part of his declared manifesto and mission announced in Luke 4.

Unfortunately, although the church should be the first place where justice is not only found, but also celebrated and lavishly distributed, it is the place where, sometimes, the opposite is true. One might begin with the time when people, striving to understand the doctrines of the church, were executed as heretics for having different views (which many today might consider benign, given some of what is proclaimed and practiced undeterred in many parts of *respectable* Christianity). Perhaps it might be the time when the Crusades were waged against Muslims. One would be quite hard pressed to imagine Jesus sanctioning any of these.

Later, the church remained silent, perhaps even complicit, while Nazism killed six million Jews. Sometime before that, the church shrugged its shoulders at slavery. On the Cape Coast of Ghana, West Africa, lies a huge property, now a tourist attraction, which includes a massive dungeon where captured Africans were held after their last bath, awaiting the ships that would transport them through the awful Middle Passage. Within walking distance from that dungeon is the ocean and a huge gateway with heavy doors, labeled "The Door of No Return." The tour guide painstakingly repeats that these human beings were held there, living in their own urine, perspiration, vomit, feces, menstruation fluids, and pus. Pointing to the cavity way up above, he indicates that the captors would throw through that opening, the food and water that these human beings were to consume—right there in the midst of their waste. The remarkable thing about this dungeon is that, when one emerges from it, back to level land and light, the marvelous beauty of the great fortress wall around it awaits. Beyond the wall is the magnificent Atlantic. Yet, amid this beauty, there is a harrowing sight: it is a chapel that sits so close to the dungeon that it would have been impossible for its worshippers not to have heard the cries of those human beings below.

The morass and ripples of slavery and the slave trade crossed the Atlantic and crossed the centuries too, buoyed by the church when it failed to stand for and generate justice. Even though emancipation in Jamaica had already been in effect for seven years, and the American version was still almost two decades away, a major split took place in a major American denomination, over a major disagreement. In 1845 the Southern Baptist Convention was born as it broke away from the American Baptists over their disagreement that they (the southerners) had not the right to possess slaves. The Southern Baptist Convention eventually apologized one hundred fifty years later for this ugly blot. Yet, they still had great difficulty, during their 2017 convention in Phoenix, in passing a resolution against the alt-right and racism and in support of the idea that black lives matter (too). In recent times, injustice in church shows up in different ways. The criminal abuse of children by trusted priests and pastors has left a massive scar not just on people but on the church itself. When it is not children, it is other forms of sexual misconduct that betrays trust and takes advantage of the vulnerable.

But there are more subtle forms of injustice that thrive in churches. Many pastors know this injustice. The attrition rate from the pastoral profession is alarming. Pastoral dismissals in some traditions is almost a contagion. As well, the attrition rate from church membership is even more alarming, given the immeasurable number of persons who have "checked out" from churches because they feel they have been injured by someone there. Church leaders and church members should be careful not to be found demanding that wronged persons forgive their offenders, while failing to demand confession, restitution, and correction from the offenders. Time and again, church people fail to follow through even with the measures Jesus offers in Matt 18:15–17, or which Paul offers in Gal 6:1, for dealing with misbehavior, injuries, and offenses in the church.

All of this signals a lack of leadership, and certainly, a failure to rise to the standard of Jesus, whose focus was the oppressed. A big question arises, then: if churches are unwilling (for they should be *able*) to manage justice within, how shall they rise to the responsibility of leading justice without? The church is not to be an end in itself; it is meant to continue the ministry of Jesus in the world (as he commands in Matt 28:18–20, but also with his focus and purpose in Luke 4:16–21). If this is so, and the church then fails to be immersed and engaged in seeking justice—jubilee—for all, to declare good news to all, and seek liberation, enlightenment, and liberation for all, then is not the church leading the world into dysfunction? What could Jesus have meant by saying to the church that it is the light of the world and the salt of the earth, when remembered in the context of these two great commissions?

The truth is that interpretations of the great commission in Matthew have too often limited congregational mission. Those interpretations limit leadership involvement in the world that upholds the church as a leader and champion of justice, just like Jesus was. Juxtaposing the *Jesus Manifesto* (Luke 4) with the great commission in Matthew 28 may enable interpretations of the great commission that might, instead, liberate congregational mission. Such interpretations might also liberate churches to make the difference they should, with the poor, the imprisoned, the blind, the oppressed, and those intentionally deprived of constant and perpetual jubilee so desperately needed. The failure of the church to make that difference contributes to making the world more and more dangerous. No more can the church be preoccupied with just its own people, parishioners, programs, property, possessions, prosperity, and prominence. The focus on prosperity and a personal salvation that maximizes the individual while mangling the community is a sign of the church being led into dysfunction. The clamor for "my blessing," and the idea of church being about Sunday only, or "a good time in worship," tell a woeful story that we may have been led into dysfunction.

But while all of this persists, the world awaits the church's leadership in the tradition, example, and name of Jesus. If the church follows that leader, Jesus, who announced that the Spirit of the Lord is upon him, then the church must reckon with what, and for what, it means that Pentecost has come upon it! If the church would renew itself to pursue impactful leadership in the world, it must imitate the example of Jesus in Luke 4. It must bring good news to the poor (through engaging in work that challenges poverty), interrupt systems that create captivity and oppression, and establish perpetual jubilee in the world. Awaiting the church in the world are scenarios crying out for leadership that pursues human dignity and justice for many, which is part and parcel of the salvation of souls. The church must understand its great commission as broader than making disciples in some limited spiritual, "churchy" way; instead, it must revisit the poor, imprisoned, captives, oppressed, dispossessed, and outcast whom Jesus sought and saved back then, and must ask who these might be in our time.

Could they be women and girls whom men won't stop harassing, abusing, or trafficking for sex? Could they be the women whom many parts of the church still oppress, denying them the exercise of their leadership gifts with which they have been endowed by their Creator? Could they be the people of different sexual orientation and identity, still deeply misunderstood and terribly unwelcome to many parts of the church? Or what about those who are different, not because of sexuality, but because of their religion (they could be Muslim, perhaps, and abused simply due to that fact), or their nationality (they could be Mexican, perhaps, and accused simply due to that fact), or their race (they could be black, and could be refused simply due to that fact—refused voting rights, for example, through a number of schemes including entrenched injustice, such as gerrymandering and judgments from courts); could it be any or all of these?

Maybe it is the burgeoning masses of people whose incomes are unlivable, even though they work full time for bosses whose incomes are 400 times more than theirs. Perhaps it may be the people who work to keep our streets and neighborhoods safe, or the victims who are constantly disrespected, brutalized, framed and killed by some of those protectors, called police, who give the honest ones a bad name. Or perhaps, it might be a whole nation, in some far flung part of the world, whose refugees or situations that create refugees do not keep us awake at nights or touch our hearts when we see their images in the news.

This passage from the book of Isaiah, which Jesus reads in the temple, is—whether we like it or recognize it or not—a *political* manifesto as much as it is a missional and salvific one. Yet, Jesus was no politician. Politics, long before it devolves into *partisan* politics, is about the distribution of wealth, resources, services, and power. Politics, therefore, often involves the *abuse* of power, causing anything ranging from imbalance to injustice; from corruption in the appropriation or distribution of those resources and services to oppression. Perhaps if congregations and church organizations understood politics in this way, they may understand the gospel and their engagement in the world differently. Perhaps they might develop an interest in victims, suffering the abuse of power and the ensuing injustice. Can such congregations seriously consider their work done by looking only at the victims and ministering to them? Shall they not be moved to challenge, also, the people and systems that deny such victims *their* Year of Jubilee? Is not all this leadership too? If all of this is leadership, then the answer to the overarching question—whom do churches lead?—is simple. Churches are led first, by Jesus Christ, and secondly, by leaders who, presumably, follow the example of Jesus, and embrace the best practices that leadership studies offer. Because churches follow not merely the example of Jesus, but the Christ himself, churches must understand that they are called to lead the oppressed out of oppression, the poor out of poverty, the imprisoned out of imprisonment, and the outcast into welcome. Then—because that constitutes only half of their work—they are to lead those who *cause* the injustices that lead to poverty, imprisonment, oppression, exclusion, and the delay, postponement, or denial of jubilee, out of *their* blindness, *their* imprisonment, and *their* callousness or wickedness. This was the work of the prophets—Amos, Hosea, Isaiah, Jeremiah, and others—before Jesus; and this was Jesus's message and mission. Luke 4:16–21 demonstrably shows that salvation is not limited to "soul" and "heaven"; it attends, also, to social realities, social constructs, and sin that is entrenched in the here and now, in the social systems of the world. Given our world today, there is much salvation to be wrought; and the many victims, as well as engineers of these sins, await the churches' power—the very power of Jesus the Christ within them—to lead them. These are those whom churches lead.

The church is a living institution. It is both organism and organization. As the life and body of Christ, it belongs to him and is meant to look like him. As an organization, it must pursue the best principles that it can discover of human and organic organization and of leadership. When the church does that, it embraces better-equipped leadership that avoids leading not only the faithful, but also the world, into dysfunction.

Appendix 1

Collaborative Performance Review Document #1

Congregational Evaluation Sheet

Name of Church _____

Evaluation Period ____/____/_____ to ____/____/_____
                 MM   DD   YYYY   MM   DD   YYYY

This evaluation sheet facilitates the evaluation of the congregation regarding their performance in and accomplishment of ministry in the church's life during the period under review. In keeping with the church's values statement, mission statement, and list of member expectations, you shall evaluate the congregation's performance.

Instructions

1. A copy of this sheet is to be completed, on behalf of the congregation, by any congregational committee charged with addressing matters regarding personnel, human resource, staff relations, or pastor relations.

2. A copy of this sheet is also to be completed by the pastor, on his own behalf, as he evaluates the congregation.

3. From the raw data collected from the congregation in the survey that you'd have distributed before, the committee, acting on behalf of the

congregation, may now complete the evaluation along the lines of the categories below. (Alternatively, the committee may feel it can evaluate the congregation without a previously distributed survey.)

4. From his own observations of and experiences in the congregation, the pastor is to complete a copy of this evaluation as well, also along the lines of the categories below.

5. Apply grades to each category as follows:

Grade Name	Meaning/Explanation	Grade Value
Exceptional	Standing way beyond expected performance levels	5
Excellent	Highest level of performance expected	4
Acceptable	The level at which all pastors are expected to perform	3
Uninspiring	Performance level that accomplished only the bare essentials	2
Unsatisfactory	Performance that fell beneath even the bare essentials	1

Quantitative

Does the congregation support and cooperate with the pastor to realize and accomplish the congregation's ministry? Does the membership demonstrate reasonably supportive attendance at worship services and meetings? Are they supporting the pastor in the church's ministry to the community? What percentage of the congregation is actively involved in one or more ministry groups or committees of the church?

After considering these questions, apply any comments and a grade in the scorecard below.

Qualitative

Does the congregation offer the pastor a healthy environment in which to discharge his ministry? To what degree do they offer opportunities for joy instead of sorrow? Does the congregation exude an aura of healthy spirituality, or, instead, toxicity? Do the members behave in ways that would encourage a new visitor to remain permanently?

After considering these questions, apply comments and a grade in the scorecard below.

Organizational Compliance

Do the church's members defend and support the congregation as a *covenant* community, or do they do their own thing and pursue their own agenda? To what degree do members abide by the best values of the congregation? How well do parishioners cooperate with pastor and leaders in organizing the church for ministry?

After considering these questions, apply comments and a grade in the scorecard below.

Relationships

Is the congregation genuinely warm with one another and with the pastor? Are members gracious and easy to engage? Are they welcoming and genuinely friendly towards visitors? Does the pastor feel respect and encouragement from leaders and members?

After considering these questions, apply comments and a grade in the scorecard below.

Expertise and Skills

Is there any notable effort from anywhere in the membership of persons showing deeper interest in leadership development? Are persons offering themselves more intentionally for volunteer positions of service? Have any new skills or gifts been discovered during the review period?

After considering these questions, apply comments and a grade in the scorecard below.

Scorecard

Area of Performance	Grade Name	Grade Value	Comments
Quantitative			
Qualitative			
Organizational Compliance			
Relationships			
Expertise and Skills			

Grade Tally _____ Grade Average _____

Appendix 2

Collaborative Performance Review Document #2

Pastor's Evaluation Sheet

Name of Pastor _____

Evaluation Period ____/____/_____ to ____/____/_____
                    MM   DD   YYYY   MM   DD   YYYY

This evaluation sheet facilitates the evaluation of the pastor regarding his professional performance in accomplishing ministry during the period under review. In keeping with the church's values statement, mission statement and list of pastor expectations, you shall evaluate the pastor's performance.

Instructions

1. A copy of this sheet is to be completed by the pastor himself, bearing in mind his duties, best pastoral practices, and any objectives or duties specifically mentioned in any pastor-congregational covenant, agreement, or contract.

2. A copy of this sheet is to be also completed, on behalf of the congregation, by any congregational committee charged with addressing matters regarding personnel, human resource, staff relations, or pastor relations. Information collected from the pastor evaluation survey that you'd have distributed before, would aid the committee, acting on

behalf of the congregation, to complete the evaluation. (Alternatively, the committee may feel it can adequately evaluate the pastor on the congregation's behalf, based on feedback attained otherwise without a previously distributed survey.)

3. Apply grades to each category as follows:

Grade Name	Meaning/Explanation	Grade Value
Exceptional	Standing way beyond expected performance levels	5
Excellent	Highest level of performance expected	4
Acceptable	The level at which all pastors are expected to perform	3
Uninspiring	Performance level that accomplished only the bare essentials	2
Unsatisfactory	Performance that fell beneath even the bare essentials	1

Quantitative

Did the pastor complete the various tasks expected of him—preaching, counseling, teaching, visitation, planning, leadership development, and community-building? Did he do these in reasonable frequencies? Was there a lack in any of these areas?

After considering these questions, apply comments and a grade in the scorecard below.

Qualitative

How much impact has the pastor's ministry had, in the period under review, upon the congregation and the community in which the church is situated? Is the congregation hopeful or uneasy; organized or disorganized? Does the congregation enjoy improved or declined health due to the pastor's ministry? Is the congregation challenged or bored? Do the members report or show signs of spiritual growth or stagnation or shrinkage, due to the pastor's ministry?

After considering these questions, apply comments and a grade in the scorecard below.

Organizational Compliance

How well has the pastor observed the congregation's best values? (If the congregation does not have a values statement, it should develop one, for the sake of clarity.) To what degree has he observed congregational procedures, following the best and healthiest organizational practices? How well has he organized or helped organize the church for ministry?

After considering these questions, apply comments and a grade in the scorecard below.

Relationships

Has the pastor contributed to or forged healthy relationships in the congregation and in the community? Does the pastor's interaction with members encourage productive relationships that strengthen the church's viability in the community, or does he contribute to weakening them? Do reasonable people feel at home in the congregation because of the pastor's approach, or does he push people away?

After considering these questions, apply comments and a grade in the scorecard below.

Expertise and Skills

Has the pastor improved his professional skills in the period under review? How well has he utilized, implemented or demonstrated these skills in the course of this period? Has he made her/himself more valuable to the organization during this period? Has he shown any kind of creativity or innovation? Has he stimulated new or further vision for the congregation?

After considering these questions, apply comments and a grade in the scorecard below.

Scorecard

Area of Performance	Grade Name	Grade Value	Comments
Quantitative			
Qualitative			
Organizational Compliance			
Relationships			
Expertise and Skills			

Grade Tally _____ Grade Average _____

Appendix 3

Collaborative Performance Review Document #3

The Collaborative Evaluation Meeting

This meeting is convened after congregational representatives and pastor have each completed *both* Collaborative Performance Review Documents #1 and #2; one for themselves and one for the other party. Each shall have been completed with grades and comments.

The meeting proceeds as follows:

First, the Pastor's Review

1. Beginning with the pastor's performance review documents, the congregation's representatives share their completed #2 document, expanding on any comments they have noted in the requisite column, and indicating their grades for each section. It is not necessary to proceed in the order in which the review document is laid out; instead, it may be a much better idea to target the areas where favorable comments and grades are apportioned, before going on to the less favorable. (This is known as the appreciative approach.)

2. The pastor shares his completed #2 document, expanding on any comments he has noted in the requisite column, and indicating his grades for each section. Similarly, he might take positives first, and negatives later.

3. Both parties discuss any differences between their grades and their observations. The primary objective is to celebrate what can be celebrated, and to lovingly and joyfully reflect on any matter for which either side has scored the pastor as being below satisfactory. Feedback should be as honest—but also as gracious and compassionate—as possible. Where the pastor has scored satisfactorily, the discussion might explore how that grade could possibly improve and what the congregation—not just the pastor—can do to enable him to improve.

4. Wherever the grades for each of the five categories are different, both parties should then attempt a consensus or *collaborative* grade. This could mean the pastor agreeing that he has graded himself either too low where the congregation has graded him higher, or too high where the congregation has graded him lower. Similarly, both sides might agree on an average of both grades. Or, finally, the congregation might in fact agree with the pastor's lower grade, or his higher grade, and vice-versa. The objective is to agree on the final grade, so that the celebrations, as well as the challenges for improvement, are shared by all.

Second, the Congregation's Review

1. Selecting the congregation's performance review documents, the congregation's representatives share their completed #1 document, expanding on any comments they have noted in the requisite column, and indicating their grades for each section. Here again, it is not necessary to proceed in the order in which the review document is laid out; instead, it may be a much better idea to target the areas where favorable comments and grades are apportioned, before going on to the less favorable. The pastor shares his completed #1 document, expanding on any comments he has noted in the requisite column, and indicating his grades for each section. He too, might target the positives before the negatives.

2. Both parties discuss any differences between their grades and their observations. The primary objective is to celebrate what can be celebrated, and to lovingly and joyfully reflect on any matter for which either side has scored the congregation as being below satisfactory. Feedback should be as honest—but also as gracious and compassionate—as possible. Where the congregation has scored satisfactorily, the discussion might explore how that grade could possibly improve and what the *pastor*—not just the congregation—can do to enable them to improve.

3. Wherever the grades for each of the five categories are different, both parties should then attempt a consensus or *collaborative* grade. This could mean the congregation agreeing that they have graded themselves either too low where the pastor has graded them higher, or too high where the pastor has graded them lower. Similarly, both sides might agree on an average of both grades. Or, finally, the pastor might in fact agree with the congregation's lower grade, or their higher grade and vice-versa. The objective is to agree on the final grade, so that the celebrations, as well as the challenges for improvement, are shared by all.

Third, the Next Steps

1. Discuss together, and itemize, specific steps and measures that the congregation might adopt for performance enhancement during the next review period.

2. Discuss together, and itemize, specific steps and measures that the pastor might adopt for performance enhancement during the next review period.

3. Itemize, for discussion in the next congregational meeting, matters that might require further congregational deliberation out of which a determination could better be made on what new measures the congregation could adopt.

4. Itemize, for discussion in the next council or general board meeting, matters that might require more deliberation by the church leaders, out of which new ideas and better practices for congregation and pastor might arise.

Appendix 4

Crestview Community Church Deeper Growth Ministry Logical Framework Matrix

Project Description or Narrative Summary	Performance/ Objectively Verifiable Indicators (How will we Know)	Means of Verification (How will we Show)	Assumptions
Goal/Wider Objective Encourage **all** Christians to enroll in and attend Christian Education and Discipleship development classes.	All Christians would be engaged in Christian Education and Discipleship development classes.	Churches' attendance records would show attendance at some form of Christian Education or Discipleship development event that at least matches weekly worship attendance.	

Project Description or Narrative Summary	Performance/ Objectively Verifiable Indicators (How will we Know)	Means of Verification (How will we Show)	Assumptions
Purpose/ Specific Project Objective Increase enrollment in and attendance at Crestview Baptist Church's Deeper Growth Ministry Classes to one thousand participants weekly by December, 2016.	Crestview's DGM enrollment and attendance increase to one thousand by December, 2016.	Crestview's attendance records for 2016, generated in January, 2017, would show one thousand attendees at DGM classes, versus the one hundred twenty-two of 2013.	Crestview may repeat this process to increase enrollment beyond one thousand; churches elsewhere may use this process also, to increase enrollment and attendance in their discipleship programs.
Component Objectives 1. Increase DGM teaching staff to one hundred members.	1. Scores of new faces are seen in DGM classes, and introduced as trainee teachers.	1. One hundred persons are introduced to the congregation and confirmed as DGM teachers.	1. Crestview leaders would discover and persuade scores of new persons to offer to serve as DGM teachers.
2. Equip and improve teaching skills for DGM staff.	2. Staff's teaching competencies improve.	2. Positive student reviews and evaluations of staff.	2. Staff will return with superior teaching skills.

Project Description or Narrative Summary	Performance/ Objectively Verifiable Indicators (How will we Know)	Means of Verification (How will we Show)	Assumptions
3. Pastor and other key leaders promote DGM during worship.	3. DGM promotions appear on Sundays.	3. Worshippers surveyed about impact of the promotions.	3. The promotions would be attractive and compelling.
4. Pastor and key leaders promote the DGM as a crucially necessary component of Crestview's life, development and effectiveness.	4. The promotions declare the indispensability of the DGM to Crestview's health.	4. Worshippers indicate, via surveys, a new understanding of the place of DGM in their lives.	4. Crestview members would accept that the DGM is as crucial as worship and music in Crestview's life and effectiveness.
5. Leaders attend DGM classes so as to set example of desired enrollment.	5. Crestview leaders are among the first new enrollees in the DGM.	5. Crestview leaders report on their experiences in the DGM in various leadership meetings.	5. Persons who see the leaders' example would begin attending DGM classes.
6. Crestview devotes more time, attention and resources on developing the DGM.	6. Crestview's DGM begins to receive as much attention as the music and worship.	6. Time and attendance sheets for DGM development match worship and music meetings.	6. The DGM would be given the developmental attention as Crestview's music ministry.

Project Description or Narrative Summary	Performance/ Objectively Verifiable Indicators (How will we Know)	Means of Verification (How will we Show)	Assumptions
7. Add new meeting times and places/spaces to accommodate the larger enrollment.	7. New alternative meeting times and places/spaces are announced.	7. Sign-up sheets are posted in foyer at welcome tables or available online.	7. Additional meeting times and places would lead to increased enrollment.
8. Crestview leaders do regular assessments of the DGM ministry to discern needs and trends.	8. Assessments become part of the regular language of both DGM and Crestview's general leadership.	8. Assessment reports are received DGM or Discipleship leadership meetings at least twice annually.	8. Crestview leaders grow in understanding about the true status and condition of the DGM.
Activities 1. Recruit new DGM teaching staff. *Begin by October 1, 2014*	1. Recruitment procedures, announcements and initiatives are prominent in bulletins and meetings. *Begin by November 1, 2014*	1. New teaching staff are introduced in worship and their commitment celebrated therein. *Complete by June 30, 2015*	1. There are willing and capable Crestview members who would say "yes", when invited to teach.

Project Description or Narrative Summary	Performance/ Objectively Verifiable Indicators (How will we Know)	Means of Verification (How will we Show)	Assumptions
2. Send all DGM teachers to continuing Christian education development seminars/ workshops. *Begin by June 30, 2015*	2. Training opportunities are identified for DGM teachers; teachers notified and attend. *Complete by January 2016*	2. Reports and reflections from each teacher are received by DGM leader. *Complete by July 2016*	2. Teachers willing to attend seminars/ workshops and Crestview willing to fund it.
3. Install a component in worship that calls Crestviewites to *learning* and *discipleship* with the same import it calls them to *giving*. *Complete by February 2015*	3. A promotional slot, calling all Crestview worshippers to be growing disciples, learning via the DGM, is launched. *Launch on February 1, 2015*	3. A challenge to learn and be a disciple is heard in every worship service, as is the call to giving. *Launch by February 1, 2015*	3. The audio-visual team, pastor, and leaders would work together to develop a two-minute promotional slot.
4. Encourage and require leaders to accept DGM classes as an integral part of their equipment to exercise leadership. *Complete by March 1, 2015*	4. Pastor and key Education and DGM leaders meet with all Crestview leaders to encourage this initiative of leading by example. *Begin by September 1, 2014*	4. Pastor announces to church the commitment of several (or all) Crestview leaders to enroll in DGM classes. *Announce January 11, 2015*	4. Leaders would be humble and responsible enough to accept the challenge and duty of being *learners* in order to be *leaders*.

Project Description or Narrative Summary	Performance/ Objectively Verifiable Indicators (How will we Know)	Means of Verification (How will we Show)	Assumptions
5. Increase the allocation for Crestview's DGM to substantially more than 0.7 percent of total budget. *Complete for 2015 Budget*	5. Trustees, treasurer and financial comptroller all agree on a significant increase for the DGM. *Complete September 1, 2014*	5. The budget for 2015 reveals significant increase for the DGM. *Seen in Budget 2015 Launch*	5. The trustees and DGM leaders would agree that 0.7 percent of budget is scandalously insufficient.
6a. Purchase new teacher and student materials. *Complete by October 2015*	6a. Suppliers are identified and purchase orders have been made. *Complete by August 1, 2015*	6a. Boxes of materials have arrived in the church's storage area. *Complete by October 31, 2015*	6a. There will be the "right intersection" of money and materials.
6b. Purchase equipment. *Complete by November 2015*	6b. Suppliers are identified and purchase orders have been made. *Complete by August 1, 2015*	6b. Equipment has arrived and has been installed in classrooms and/ or homes. *Complete by December 15, 2015*	6b. There will be the "right intersection" of money and equipment.

Project Description or Narrative Summary	Performance/ Objectively Verifiable Indicators (How will we Know)	Means of Verification (How will we Show)	Assumptions
7. Identify alternative meeting times and places suitable to participants, for increased attendance. *Begin by November 1, 2014*	7. Alternative meeting times and places are identified and planned by the DGM team. *Complete by August 1, 2015*	7. Alternative meeting times and places are announced and promoted around the Crestview campus. *Launch by September 1, 2015*	7. Crestview members would be willing to choose times other than Sunday and places other than Crestview.
8. Create an evaluation instrument for Crestview's DGM and execute this at least twice annually. *Begin by January 1, 2015*	8. The Crestview DGM team and other leaders develop an evaluation instrument. *Complete by March 31, 2015*	8. An evaluation instrument is delivered to Crestview's DGM leaders and is launched among the congregation. *Launch by May 1, 2015*	8. The Education ministry and other leaders would develop and disseminate this instrument to all participants.
9. Begin DGM classes with the new schedule, locations, teachers, and materials. *January 4, 2016*	9. Classes have begun by January 4, 2016.	9. Crestview's members are talking about the great new DGM!	9. All parts of this strategic plan have been put in place.

Project Description or Narrative Summary	Performance/ Objectively Verifiable Indicators (How will we Know)	Means of Verification (How will we Show)	Assumptions
10. Evaluate the progress of enrollment, and issues related thereto. *March 31, June 30, and September 30, 2016*	10. Surveys and interviews are being conducted among Crestview members.	10. Survey and interview reports are tabulated, analyzed, and reported on, to the congregation.	10. There are new developments with the DGM, and Crestview members are excited to be surveyed and interviewed about them.
11. Ascertain that enrollment and attendance have reached one thousand. *December 31, 2016*	11. A final tally is done.	11. The final tally is announced.	11. The evaluations and tally are done.
12. The congregation celebrates the one thousand milestone of DGM students. *Christmas Party or Christmas Eve Services, 2016, or before January 15, 2017.*	12. The celebration date and time is announced.	12. The celebration happens, and both it, and its *raison d'etre*, are the talk of the town!	12. The attendance at Crestview's DGM classes, during 2016, has reached one thousand participants.

Bibliography

Antonakis, John, et al. *The Nature of Leadership*. Thousand Oaks, CA: Sage, 2004.

Arbinger Institute. *Leadership and Self-Deception: Getting Out of the Box*. 2nd ed. San Francisco: Berrett-Koehler, 2010.

Avolio, Bruce J., and Bernard M. Bass. *Developing Potential Across a Full Range of Leadership: Cases on Transactional and Transformational Leadership*. Mahwah, NJ: Erlbaum Associates, 2002.

Barbeito, Carol L. *Human Resource Policies and Procedures for Nonprofit Organizations*. Hoboken, NJ: Wiley, 2004.

Bass, Bernard M. *Bass & Stogdill's Handbook of Leadership: Theory, Research, and Managerial Applications*. 3rd ed. New York: The Free Press, 1990.

Bass, Bernard M., and Paul Steidlmeier. "Ethics, Character, and Authentic Transformational Leadership Behavior." *LQ* 10 (1999) 181–217. https://umesorld.files.wordpress.com/2011/02/ethics-character-and-authentic-transformational-leadership-behavior-1999-bass-and-steidlmeier.pdf.

Blunt, Peter, and Merrick L. Jones. "Exploring the Limits of Western Leadership Theory in East Asia and Africa." *Personnel Review* 26 (1997) 6–23.

Bolman, Lee G., and Terrence E. Deal. *Reframing Organizations: Artistry, Choice, and Leadership*. 4th ed. San Francisco: Jossey-Bass, 2008.

Brueggemann, Walter. *The Prophetic Imagination*. 2nd ed. Philadelphia: Fortress, 2001.

Butler, Timothy, and James Waldroop. "Job Sculpting: The Art of Retaining Your Best People." *Harvard Business Review* (September–October 1999) 144–52.

Collingwood, Harris. "Personal Histories: Leaders Remember the Moments and People That Shaped Them." *Harvard Business Review on Breakthrough Leadership*. Boston: Harvard Business School, 2001.

Collins, Jim. *Good to Great and the Social Sectors*. New York: HarperCollins, 2005.

Eagly, Alice H., and Linda L. Carli. "The Female Leadership Advantage: An Evaluation of the Evidence." *LQ* 14 (2003) 807–34.

Everist, Norma C., and Craig L. Nessan. *Transforming Leadership: New Vision for a Church in Mission*. Minneapolis, MN: Fortress, 2008.

First African Baptist Church. "First African Baptist Church History." http://firstafricanbc.com/history.asp.

Fisher, Roger, and William Ury. *Getting to Yes*. Boston: Houghton Mifflin, 1981.

Foster, Richard J. *Money, Sex & Power: The Challenge of the Disciplined Life.* New York: HarperCollins, 1987.

The Free Believers Network. "Why Pastors Leave the Ministry". http://freebelievers.com/article/why-pastors-leave-the-ministry.

Gayle, Clement. *George Liele: Pioneer Missionary to Jamaica.* Kingston, Jamaica: The Jamaica Baptist Union, 1982.

George, Bill. *Authentic Leadership: Rediscovering the Secrets to Creating Lasting Value.* San Francisco: Jossey-Bass, 2003.

———. *True North: Discover Your Authentic Leadership.* San Francisco: Jossey-Bass, 2007.

Gill, Roger. *Theory and Practice of Leadership.* 2nd ed. London: Sage, 2011.

Goleman, Daniel. *Emotional Intelligence: Why It Can Matter More Than IQ.* 10th Anniversary ed. New York: Bantam, 2006.

———."Leadership That Gets Results." *HBR* (March–April 2000) 78–90.

Greenleaf, Robert. K. *The Servant as Leader.* Westfield, IN: The Greenleaf Center for Servant Leadership, 1991.

Gunderson, Gary. *Boundary Leaders: Leadership Skills for People of Faith.* Philadelphia: Augsburg, 2004.

Hahn, Celia Allison. *Growing in Authority: Relinquishing Control: A New Approach to Leadership.* Durham, NC: The Alban Institute, 1984.

Halliburton, John. *The Authority of a Bishop.* London: SPCK, 1987.

Heifetz, Ronald A., and Marty Linsky. *Leadership on the Line: Staying Alive Through the Dangers of Leading.* Boston, MS: Harvard Business School Press, 2002.

Hersey, Paul, et al. *Management of Organizational Behavior.* 8th ed. Upper Saddle River, NJ: Prentice Hall, 2001.

International Ministries. "A Past, Present and Future As Bright As the Promises of God." https://www.internationalministries.org/history/.

Keller, Tiffany. "Images of the Familiar: Individual Differences and Implicit Leadership Theories." *Leadership Quarterly* 10 (1999) 589-607.

Kellerman, Barbara. *Bad Leadership.* Boston, MA: Harvard Business School Press, 2004.

———. "How Bad Leadership Happens." *Leader to Leader* 35 (2005) 41–46.

———. *Leadership: Essential Selections on Power, Authority and Influence.* New York: McGraw-Hill, 2010.

Kezar, Adrianna J., et al. "Rethinking the 'L' Word in Higher Education: The Revolution of Research on Leadership." *ASHE Higher Education Report* 31 (6) New York: Jossey-Bass, 2006.

King, Martin Luther Jr. "Letter from a Birmingham Jail." https://www.africa.upenn.edu/Articles_Gen/Letter_Birmingham.html.

Kouzes, James M., and Barry Z. Posner, eds. *Christian Reflections on the Leadership Challenge.* 4th ed. San Francisco: Jossey-Bass, 2006.

Kritzinger, J. N. J. "A Question of Missions—A Mission of Questions." *Missionalia* 30 (2002) 144–73.

Lipman-Blumen, Jean. "The Allure of Toxic Leaders: Why Followers Rarely Escape Their Clutches." *Ivey Business Journal* (Jan–Feb 2005) 1–8.

Magee, David. *How Toyota Became #1: Leadership Lessons from the World's Greatest Car Company.* New York: Penguin, 2007.

Mangaliso, Mzamo. "Building Competitive Advantage from Ubuntu: Management Lessons From South Africa." *Academy of Management Executive,* 15 (2001) 23–33.

Maxwell, John C. *The 21 Irrefutable Laws of Leadership*. Nashville, TN: Thomas Nelson, 1998.

Northouse, Peter. *Leadership Theory and Practice*. 6th ed. Los Angeles: Sage, 2013.

Nouwen, Henri J. M. *In the Name of Jesus: Reflections on Christian Leadership*. New York: Crossroad, 1989.

"Pastor Burnout Statistics." http://www.pastorburnout.com/pastor-burnout-statistics. html.

Pearce, Terry. *Leading Out Loud: Inspiring Change through Authentic Communication*. San Francisco: Jossey-Bass. 2003.

Posavac, Emil J. *Program Evaluation: Methods and Case Studies*. 8th ed. Upper Saddle River, NJ: Prentice Hall, 2010.

Pynes, Joan E. *Human Resource Management for Public and Nonprofit Organizations*. 3rd ed. San Francisco: Jossey-Bass, 2004.

Rosen, Robert, and Patricia Digh. "Developing Globally Literate Leaders." *Training and Development* (May 2001). http://www.thierryschool.be/solar-system/starship-II/artemis/8AbraTefadu.pdf.

Rost, Joseph C. *Leadership for the Twenty-First Century*. Westport, CT: Praeger, 1991.

Russell, Horace O. *The Baptist Witness: A Concise Baptist History*. El Paso: Baptist Spanish Publishing House, 1983.

Sawhill, John C., and David Williamson. "Mission Impossible? Measuring Success in Nonprofit Organizations." *Nonprofit Management & Leadership* 11 (2001) 371–86.

Senge, Peter. M. *The Fifth Discipline: The Art and Practice of the Learning Organization*. New York: Broadway Business, 2006.

Smith, Shawn, and Rebecca Mazin. *The HR Answer Book: An Indispensable Guide for Managers and Human Resources Professionals*. New York: AMACOM, 2004.

Sosik, John J., and Dongli I. Jung. *Full-Range Leadership Development: Pathways for People, Profit and Planet*. New York: Routledge, 2010.

Spears, Larry. C., and Michele Lawrence. *Focus on Leadership: Servant-Leadership for the Twenty-First Century*. New York: Wiley and Sons, 2002.

Stewart, G. Bennett, et al., "Rethinking Rewards." *Harvard Business Review* (Nov–Dec 1993) 3–11.

Yukl, Gary. "An Evaluation of Conceptual Weaknesses in Transformational and Charismatic Leadership Theories." *LQ* 10 (1999) 285–305.

Zaleznik, Abraham. "Managers and Leaders: Are They Different?" *Best of HBR* (1977) 74–81.